THE GIRL GUIDES
1910—1970

ALIX LIDDELL is the daughter of Rose Kerr, the first Chairman of
the World Committee, and has given many years' service to Guiding
in her own right. As well as being the author of several publications,
she is Editor of *The Council Fire*, the quarterly magazine of the
World Association. She was awarded the O.B.E. in the 1970 Birthday
Honours.

The Chief Guide in Manitoba during her visit to Canada in 1962

THE GIRL GUIDES
1910–1970

Alix Liddell

FREDERICK MULLER

First published in Great Britain in 1956 by
Frederick Muller Limited, Fleet Street, London, E.C.4
Reprinted 1957, 1958, 1959, 1961, 1962
Revised 1965
Reprinted 1966
New Edition, Completely Revised, 1970

Typesetting by Print Origination, Liverpool
Litho printed by Redwood Press Ltd.
Bound by Wm. Brendon & Son Ltd.
SBN: 584 62019 5

Contents

Illustrations

Baden-Powell

The Boy

A RED-HEADED schoolboy crouched over a "hunter's" fire in a clearing in a copse. He had cut away the turf before laying the fire and now he was feeding it with smallish dry twigs, taking care to keep it tiny and bright with no tell-tale smoke to give him away, for as usual he was breaking bounds. Presently he started skinning the rabbit he had snared, preparatory to making a meal of it. He seemed absorbed in his task but his ears were cocked to catch the slightest sound. A moment later he heard it—the cracking of a twig as somebody entered the wood. Quick as a flash he seized the sod, clamped it down on the fire and stamped it into position; the rabbit was thrust into a previously prepared hiding place under a bush; then he swung himself up into the branches of a nearby tree and lay silently peering down through the leaves at the schoolmaster who presently emerged and strolled across the clearing.

The boy had already discovered that few people look upwards even when searching for somebody—a discovery that many years later was to play a not insignificant part in the founding of the Boy Scout Movement; for the freckled lad who on this occasion shinned so nimbly up a tree was Robert Stephenson Smyth Baden-Powell, more commonly known as "Bathing Towel" at Charterhouse School where he was then a pupil.

His home name was "Ste", but to millions of boys and girls of future years he was to be known as "The Chief Scout" or "The Founder" or simply as "B.-P."

B.-P. used to say that he learnt his first lesson in military tactics when the school was still in London. A fight was in progress between the boys of the school and the boys of the town, and the Charterhouse boys were getting the worst of it. Just then the Headmaster appeared.

"Go through there," he said, pointing at a door in the wall of the school yard, "and take them in the flank."

"But the door's locked, sir," said B.-P.

"Yes, but I have the key," replied the Head, producing it from his pocket . . . and in this way the town boys were routed.

Soon after this incident the school moved from its original site to Surrey. B.-P. loved the new-found freedom of the country where he was always more at home than in the streets of a town, and spent much of his time in somewhat unorthodox pursuits, as we have seen.

He was not, like his eldest brother Warington, a fine scholar, but he left his mark on the school as an agreeable eccentric who was often at the bottom of some schoolboy prank, as for instance when he was suddenly called on to fill a gap in a school concert and gave a brilliant impromptu impersonation of the French master, to the huge delight of the boys, and indeed of the master himself.

His gift for mimicry and his talent for disguise stood him in good stead when he became a soldier, enabling him on one occasion to spend two days in the enemy's camp in India as a half-witted tramp while he collected vitally impórtant information. But it got him into trouble, too, for he could not resist dressing up and playing jokes on his brother officers, pretending perhaps to be a pompous personage visiting the mess, and when they found out how they had been deceived they naturally paid him back with a ragging—but it was all done in good fun, even if somewhat roughly!

B.-P. was born in 1857, the fourth of a family of five sons and one daughter. His father, a clergyman and a scholar, died when he was a small boy leaving Mrs. Baden-Powell to bring up this large family with very little money.

She herself was a woman of character and ability, and she expected her children to cultivate their various talents. Ste's first letter to her from boarding school was returned with the comment that it was not what she expected of him, for it had no illustrations. After that his home letters were liberally dotted with pen-and-ink sketches, and he became in time a very accomplished artist, himself illustrating the books he wrote later on, whether with comical sketches or with water-colour paintings.

Where Mrs. Baden-Powell differed from most other Victorian parents was in the encouragement she gave to her boys to go off on their own in the holidays, exploring the countryside and fending for themselves.

In those days of course there was no radio, television or cinema, and families were obliged to make their own entertainment (especially where there was no spare cash left over after paying the school fees) or sit about and get bored.

The Baden-Powell family was never bored. The four oldest brothers would go off for a tramping holiday, sleeping in the open, or in a barn if it were wet. When they reached a town they always asked to be shown over the local factory, or else they went sightseeing, filling the log-book they kept of each trip with sketches of churches and castles. In this way they collected a lot of information about various trades and industries, and learnt a good deal of history.

Sometimes instead of tramping they took their home-made canoe and paddled up the Thames as far as they could go. Once they went all the way to its source, "portaged" the canoe over the Cotswolds and paddled on down into Wales.

Later on they saved up enough money to buy an old whaler, and in this they sailed all round the coast of Great Britain, and once even went to Norway. Coming back they ran into a storm, and the four brothers might well have gone down with their ship had it not been for Warington's magnificent seamanship, added to the splendid discipline of his crew. The younger boys learnt then that swiftness and efficiency in obeying an order meant the difference between coming safely into harbour and finishing their careers at the bottom of the North Sea.

Nobody knows how they came out of all their escapades alive, but all the time they were learning—learning how to work as a team, learning how to fend for themselves, learning the secrets of the countryside and of the sea—learning many things that are not taught in school.

Sometimes they learnt the hard way.

One day Ste was told to prepare the dinner. It was not a great success. Indeed, the result was quite horrible and nobody could be expected to eat it. Nobody? His three brothers thought otherwise, and forced him to eat every scrap of the unappetizing mess himself. After that he learnt to cook almost overnight.

The Soldier

B.-P. left school with no idea of what he was going to do in life. He went up to Balliol College, Oxford, for an interview with the famous Master, Dr. Jowett, who pronounced him "not quite up to Balliol form"—or did he mean Baden-Powell form, for his brother had won a scholarship?

Shortly afterwards he saw in *The Times* a notice of an examination for direct commissions into the army. He had not previously thought of the army as a career, but on the whim of the moment he decided to sit for the examination, though he did not fancy his chances of passing.

Some weeks later he was yachting with a friend who happened to pick up a newspaper and look idly down the list of successful candidates.

"I see here," he said, "that a Baden-Powell has done very well in this army exam. Any relation of yours?"

B.-P. looked over his shoulder and to his amazement saw that it was none other than himself. He was fourth out of seven hundred candidates, and had been placed second for the cavalry.

Now in those days an army officer was expected to have some money of his own apart from his pay, which did not amount to much; it was not thought that a young subaltern, especially in the cavalry, could support himself and his horses without an allowance from his parents. B.-P., however, felt that it would not be fair to ask his mother to help him. She had already had a struggle to pay for her children's education, and he thought she was now entitled to a little comfort for herself and less worry about money matters.

He determined, therefore, that he would live on his pay, and since pay was higher in India than in England he asked to be sent to the East immediately.

Normally a young man entering the army went to the Royal Military College, Sandhurst, as an officer-cadet before joining a regiment, but the first six in this particular examination were excused this preliminary training, and so it happened that within a few weeks of settling on a career B.-P. was on his way to India.

Although he was determined to live on his pay he was equally determined to enjoy himself. Polo, pig-sticking and shooting were all to be included in his programme. Later on he thought that stalking animals in order to photograph or sketch them was better than to kill them, but as a young officer, sport was an important part of life, even if expensive. He managed to pay his way partly by economizing—no smoking, for instance—and partly by making money through buying "raw" ponies, schooling them and selling them at a profit as "made" polo ponies. His appearance on the polo ground on one of his half-trained animals was not greeted with enthusiasm by his brother officers—it tended to turn the game into a sort of circus—but B.-P. didn't care—he was enjoying himself immensely.

With all this he took his soldiering very seriously. War in the nineteenth century was very different from what it became in the twentieth. There were no tanks, no atomic bombs, no aeroplanes, no "walkie-talkie" sets. Reconnaissance of the enemy's position was carried out by scouts either on horseback or on foot, and a young officer in command of a company might be out on his own, cut off from all communication with his headquarters for days, or even weeks, at a time. He alone would be responsible for the success of the expedition and the lives of his men.

B.-P. practised stalking and tracking assiduously and became the best scout in the army. He was constantly being sent out to discover what the war-like tribes on the frontier were planning, for they frequently used to raid the army posts, generally to carry off horses. B.-P. always kept his kit packed in readiness to set off on an expedition, so that when he was asked, "Can you be ready to leave in two hours' time?" his answer was invariably, "Sir, I can go now!"

He was also very concerned with the welfare of his men. The recruits joining the regiment were good lads, but lacking in initiative, and this worried B.-P. Having no hobbies to amuse them in their leisure time, they were constantly getting into trouble through the boredom that led them into foolish scrapes. They had little sense of responsibility and no idea of the qualities needed in a good soldier, such as observation, the team spirit and the ability to look after himself in strange country.

B.-P., looking back on his own boyhood, felt sorry for these lads who had never had the opportunities for adventure which he had enjoyed with his brothers, and he determined to hand on to them some of the fun they had so far missed, and at the same time turn them into soldiers worthy of the traditions of the regiment.

With these aims in mind he started training them as scouts—sending them out to explore the country round about. They would be away for a few days at a time and had to camp, procure and cook their own food and generally look after themselves in unknown territory. Most important of all they had to bring back a report of all they had seen and heard, and any deductions they had drawn from it. This meant that they had to learn to observe intelligently, to note the tracks of beasts and men and discover, through apparently insignificant details, where they were going and why.

As a rule the men went out in couples; but a particularly stupid fellow was always sent alone, so that he had to rely on himself and not on his companion.

Later on, when B.-P. was Colonel of his regiment, he designed a badge which was awarded to every man who showed himself sufficiently competent. This emblem was the sign which signifies "North" on a compass: the arrow-head. It was eventually adopted officially by the army as the badge of a qualified scout, and later still it became the badge of the Boy Scouts.

B.-P. had plenty of experience in scouting when engaged in the wars against the Ashanti and Matabele—two African tribes which were causing much trouble to the Dutch and British settlers by raiding their farms, burning their buildings, carrying off their livestock and often killing their families.

No doubt B.-P. enjoyed the thrill of pitting his wits against the enemy, whom he always looked upon as honourable and brave opponents; but he hated war, and always took the first opportunity of turning his foes into friends and arranging a peaceful settlement of any quarrel.

He himself gained the respect of his opponents, who named him Impeesa—"The wolf that never sleeps"—and when the fighting was over he also gained their affection. He came to love Africa very dearly, and towards the end of his long life he made it his home.

The Hero

It was May 1900, and all England had gone mad. In London throughout the night crowds jostled through the streets, singing, shouting and waving flags. A new expression came into the language, to "Maffick", meaning "to exult riotously".

The crowd 'mafficks' in Piccadilly, 1900

The cause of all this was the news that Mafeking had at last been relieved.

You can read in your history books about the war between the British and the South African people of Dutch descent, known as Boers. It is a war that should never have been fought, but this is not the place to go into the causes that led up to it.

It has been called the last "gentlemen's war" because

it was the last fight between soldiers using the old-fashioned weapons and more or less recognized rules. Civilians for instance were not deliberately killed, as in the bombing raids of subsequent wars, and on the whole both sides behaved with chivalry towards each other.

Mafeking was an isolated town with a garrison of seven hundred British soldiers, and it fell to the lot of Colonel Baden-Powell to defend it against the Boers. It would not have appeared a difficult place to capture by storm, but B.-P. had built up such a reputation for cunning that the attackers approached it with the greatest caution, not certain what "that fellow" might not spring on them. If they had known how lightly it was defended they could have walked into it any day, but B.-P. used all his wits to make them believe that it was strongly held. He ordered a "minefield" to be laid around the town. Actually there was only enough dynamite for one mine, and the other little mounds made by the soldiers were quite harmless, but the enemy did not know that. The deception was complete when a man bicycled through the minefield (against orders) and chanced to ride over the one real mine and was killed.

A searchlight was made from an old acetylene lamp and a sheet of tin. Under cover of darkness it was rushed from place to place to give the impression of a whole battery.

By a "gentlemen's agreement" between the two sides there was no fighting on Sundays, and the people of Mafeking could safely walk about outside the town, but B.-P. made them climb over imaginary barbed wire whenever they went out or came in.

So the siege went on month after month, and the people in the town grew weaker and weaker as the stocks of food dwindled. To spare the garrison unnecessary work B.-P. formed a messenger corps of quite young boys to take over certain duties. They were divided into patrols of six under a boy leader, and did much useful work as orderlies and "lookouts", and in carrying messages from one part of the town to another. They were brave and cheerful, too. One lad rode through a hail of bullets on his bicycle to deliver his despatch and was told off by B.-P. for recklessness. The cheeky young imp simply replied, "I pedalled so fast, sir, that the bullets couldn't possibly catch up with me!"

This was the future Chief Scout's first experiment with training boys, and it proved that they could be relied on to a much greater extent than most grown-ups seemed to think.

With the arrival of fresh troops the seven-month siege came to an end; the Boers were dispersed and food was brought to the starving population. B.-P., after months of duty elsewhere, returned home to find himself famous as "The Hero of Mafeking".

In England the shops were selling souvenir "buttons" bearing the portraits of one or another of the famous British soldiers taking part in the war . . . Redvers Buller, George White, Herbert Plumer and so on. A certain little girl went shopping one day to buy a button of her particular hero. She had no doubt who he was—Baden-Powell. She was twelve years old and her name was Olave Soames. She little thought then what the future held for herself and the defender of Mafeking.

It was not many months before B.-P. was on his way back to South Africa with instructions to raise a new corps; but this new corps was not for the purpose of fighting: it was to preserve the peace now that the unhappy war was over. It was called the South African Constabulary.

It may be imagined with what eagerness General Baden-Powell set about his task. At last he had a free hand to recruit, equip and train a body of men according to his own ideas. It was a wonderful opportunity to put into practice the fruits of his experience, and he set about training his recruits in the scouting method that he had found so successful in the past.

He adopted a comfortable and practical uniform, suited to the country in which the Constabulary had to work. It consisted of a bush-shirt, neckerchief, wideawake hat, and either riding breeches or shorts, according to the duty being carried out. It was a mounted corps, and B.-P. expected every man to look after his own horse and consider its welfare before his own.

The men themselves chose their motto to match the initials of their chief—Be Prepared.

It was from this fine corps, the South African Constabulary, that the Boy Scouts inherited their uniform and their motto.

The Scout

In 1899 the War Office had published a handbook for the use of army officers called *Aids to Scouting,* by Colonel R.S.S. Baden-Powell.

Although she was not an army officer, the book was

read by Miss Charlotte Mason, Principal of Ambleside, a training college for governesses.

She was much impressed by the idea of scouting as a means of fostering initiative and reliability and thought it might very easily be adapted and introduced into the education of children. She therefore placed *Aids to Scouting* on the list of books to be studied by her pupils in 1905.

One of these pupils, having completed her training, was engaged by a General as governess to his small boy.

One day as the General was riding home from some army exercises he was startled by an excited child's voice calling out, "Father, you're shot!"

He looked around but could not make out where the voice came from, until his son dropped down from the branches of a tree.

"Don't you know, Father," he said, "that you should always look up as well as around? You walked right into my ambush!"

The General was very much surprised, but he was even more surprised when the new governess also descended from the tree.

She explained the modern system for training children in alertness and observation, and told how they had stalked him on more than one occasion and had lured him away in order to creep into his study and take away some small object to prove their skill.

When this story got about in army circles B.-P. was terribly ragged; but it gave him an idea. If such a well-known teacher as Miss Mason had taken up his scheme, might there not be something in the idea of scouting for boys—as well as for men? He turned the matter over in his mind and consulted his friend Sir

William Smith, the founder and chief of the Boys Brigade, who encouraged him to go ahead and write a book adapting the scheme of training for boys. He thought it might well be used in his own organization.

B.-P. was a very practical man, and he decided that before publishing anything he must try out his theories and see if they worked.

He had a notion that it did not matter where a boy came from—from the town or the country, from a well-to-do family or a poor one, from a public school or a council school—the mere fact that boys were boys was enough to bring them together in a common liking for the same kind of adventurous activities.

This was a somewhat unusual point of view at the beginning of the twentieth century when class distinctions were fairly rigid, but B.-P. wanted to see if he were right. So he collected together a good mixed bunch of boys and took them to camp on Brownsea Island in Poole Harbour. This was in August, 1907.

The boys slept under canvas, cooked their own food and played scouting games. They were divided into patrols, and each patrol grew into a close little knot of friends, determined in good-natured rivalry to out-do the others.

The boys had a wonderful time—but perhaps B.-P. had an even more wonderful time watching all his theories work out successfully. He had no doubts left, and immediately the camp was over he finished writing his famous book *Scouting for Boys*.

He intended it to be used by already existing organizations, like the Boys Brigade, clubs, church groups and the rest, for he did not at this time mean to start a new movement, but as the book was published in

fortnightly parts at 3d. a time—the first instalment
appearing in January 1908—almost every boy in the
country could afford to buy it, and thousands did who
were not attached to any kind of organized group. They
got together in patrols and chose an animal such as a
tiger or antelope for their crest; they met in woods and
fields, in parks and back gardens; they wriggled through
the undergrowth on their tummies and swung about in
the branches of trees like monkeys; they built fires and
bridges and outdoor shelters, and pored over each
successive number of "The Book" to find out what
came next. "Scouting" evidently provided a badly
needed outlet for adventurous spirits all over the country.

The enthusiasm was tremendous, and B.-P. realized
that if the whole thing were not to get out of hand he
would have to set up some kind of organization to cope
with the astonishing outburst of activity.

It was thus that the Boy Scout Movement came into
being.

The adventurous spirits, however, were not confined
to boys. To his dismay B.-P. found himself swamped
with letters from girls begging him to allow them to be
'Boy" Scouts. "We can ride and swim and climb a tree
and track a man", wrote two sisters. "But when you
write back please don't say anything about sewing and
lessons and housework, because these are the things
Mother says we should do, and we hate them."

The Chief Scout was inclined to agree with "Mother".
He had never foreseen the game he had invented for
boys appealing to their sisters, and in the beginning he
gave them no encouragement.

But there came a day when he could no longer resist
the eager, pleading faces of the girls.

Girls Take to Scouting

The Crystal Palace Rally

The Chief Scout once said that he had only to appear at a rally for the skies to open in a deluge of rain. "Chief's weather" it came to be called amongst Scouts, and the fashion was set at the very first rally ever held. This took place at the Crystal Palace, London, in September, 1909, barely two years after the Brownsea Island camp.

If anyone still doubted the appeal of scouting to the boys of the United Kingdom he would have been convinced by the numbers who poured into the Crystal Palace on that wet September day.

Nowadays a big gathering of this kind would be planned at least a year beforehand: committees would be set up, instructions sent out to troops, arrangements made for transport and publicity. In 1909, however, the Chief Scout just "let it be known" that he would be at the Crystal Palace to meet any boys who were playing the new game . . . and 11,000 turned up!

He was astonished and delighted at so wonderful a response to his invitation. Astonished, too—though perhaps not quite so delighted—when at the tail of the march past there appeared a little posse of girls dressed in jerseys, scout hats and neckerchiefs, and carrying poles. Except for their skirts and long hair they were indistinguishable from their brothers.

The girl 'boy scouts' marching past at the Crystal Palace rally in 1909

After inspecting the boys B.-P. went over to the girls. "Who are you?" he asked. You can imagine his broad grin, for he did not really need to be told, "We are the Girl Scouts". He knew when he saw them there that he would have to give in; the girls had proved by their spirit of determination that they were not going to be left out, 6,000 of them having already registered as "Boy Scouts" with no encouragement from anybody.

B.-P. was a wise man, and maybe he realized then that it was no use training up a fine lot of boys if there were no fine girls to be their companions; so he accepted the girls, accepted them ungrudgingly, and thereafter gave them his help and advice equally with the boys.

There was one thing, however, that he decided on at once—a change of name. He knew that the boys disliked their sisters aping them and he thought they would more readily accept the girls if they had a name of their own. So in the Scout Headquarters Gazette for November, 1909, there appeared "The Scheme for 'Girl Guides'—A suggestion for Character Training for Girls".

The scheme followed very much the same lines as that for the Boy Scouts, only "differing in detail to suit the sex".

There was no need, B.-P. pointed out, "to make tomboys of refined girls", and the emphasis in training was on the more womanly pursuits such as nursing, cooking and ambulance work. He thought the Girl Guides might serve as "a feeder or cadet branch to the Territorial Organization of Voluntary Aid and Red Cross Society", but the main object was "to give them all the ability to be better mothers and Guides to the next generation". There was, however, a mention towards the end of "camp for the efficients" as "the great incentive to effort and the opportunity of really getting hold of the girls".

The excitement of the girls in being recognized by The Chief was tempered with dismay when they learnt of the feminine role assigned to them. They had no desire whatever to be "Guides to the next generation"; they wanted to be Scouts now. It was some consolation when B.-P. pointed to the regiment of Guides in India as worthy namesakes. They were the handymen of the army, he said, and prepared to tackle any job that came their way.

All the same it was difficult for the self-styled "Buffaloes" and "Wild Cats" to resign themselves to becoming "Lilies-of-the-Valley" and modest "Violets"; more difficult still to bring themselves to invite "a lady" to join their ranks as "an officer". What did ladies know about scouting?

It was some time, therefore, before all the former Girl Scouts made up their minds to become Guides, but nearly all of them eventually decided that it was best to do as their Chief suggested. Regretfully they returned their Scout badges (which they had obtained by the simple expedient of signing their applications with initials instead of Christian names, to conceal their sex) and with as good a grace as possible pinned on "the pretty trefoil" that had been designed for them.

B.-P. was too busy organizing the Scouts in 1909 to spare time to do the same for the Guides, so he asked his sister, Agnes Baden-Powell, to take the new young Association under her wing, which she was very pleased to do. A Committee of Ladies was formed from among the Baden-Powells' personal friends and the task of bringing order out of the existing chaos was taken in hand.

Early in 1910 a room in Scout Headquarters was rented as an office and registrations were taken over from the boys' department. It was then found that there were already 8,000 Guides in the United Kingdom—quite a considerable number, but nothing combared with the estimated strength of 100,000 Boy Scouts.

Hats, Poles and Brickbats

The first official uniform as laid down in "The Scheme for 'Girl Guides' " was described as: "Jersey of

company colour. Neckerchief of company colour.
Skirt, knickers, stockings, dark blue.
Cap—red biretta, or in summer large straw hat.
Haversack, cooking billy, lanyard and knife, walking
stick or light staff.
Cape hooked up on the back.
Shoulder knot of the 'Group' colour on left shoulder.
Badges, much the same as the Boy Scouts.
Officers wear ordinary country walking dress, with
biretta of dark blue, white shoulder knot, walking stick,
and whistle on lanyard."

Up to this time the different groups had designed
their own uniforms and many continued to wear these
for several years to come. Very splendid they were, too.
Scout hats turned up at the side with a bunch of cock's
feathers were popular, and so were white haversacks
with immense red crosses. Some companies wore green,
some navy blue trimmed with red or white braid, and
some khaki. Tam-o'-shanters were stuffed with paper to
make them stick up stiffly from the head in contrast to
the "straw sailors" which were inclined to droop about
the face after exposure in all weathers. But whatever the
variations in style every true Guide carried a stout pole,
marked off in feet and inches.

The main purpose of this formidable weapon was to
enable one to jump dykes, but it also came in handy for
making a stretcher or holding back crowds. As one was
never certain when one might not come across a dyke,
or (joyful thought) be present at an accident, a proper
Guide never moved a yard without her pole. Many
companies had drum and bugle bands so that all might
know when the Guides were on parade.

In some town districts it needed a good deal of

courage to march down the streets in uniform. Small
boys would run along beside the Guides making
cat-calls and even throwing brick-bats, and grown-ups
would frequently make loud and uncomplimentary
remarks about "tomboys".

On the other hand, the meetings were so enthralling
that it was well worth running the gauntlet to take part
in them.

Here is an account of one from Scotland:

"The normal procedure was as follows:

The Guides assembled outside Venlaw front door,

B.-P. inspects Girl Scouts at Brighton in 1910

soon after lunch. The captains were given sealed orders for the day; each patrol then went off on a different activity; both inside and outside the house; to make beds and have a sick-nurse talk; to light fires (indoor and out); to have some sense-training competition such as smelling; to harness the ponies; to learn to use the telephone between the house and the stables.

Each Guide brought her own food and each one possessed a billy-can; each patrol made its own tea, which was sometimes eaten all together and sometimes separately, often as part of some scouting game. The company generally had drill or country dancing as a whole to finish up with; as the evenings grew longer so did the time of dismissal, and in the summer time they often did not break up until 8 o'clock."

Most companies met out of doors and a favourite theme was "Bringing in the wounded". This involved improvising stretchers on the "battlefield", bandaging the "wounded", signalling for help, making tea, and finally—most likely—parading through the town with the "casualties".

No wonder the meetings occupied the best part of a whole Saturday!

The Dangers of Camping

Although B.-P. had talked about "camping as an incentive" the general opinion amongst grown-ups was that this was far too dangerous for girls. Camping under canvas, that is; camping in an empty house might be allowed. Even as late as 1913 Headquarters issued a warning against the dangers of allowing girls to sleep in tents.

Most of the early camps, therefore, took place with a

solid roof overhead, though the cooking was often done out of doors. Even this, however, was exciting and adventurous, because it was something new for most girls, who then had nothing like the freedom that is considered quite normal to-day.

It was a rather nerve-racking experience for a Captain, when you consider that there was no camp training for her to attend in order to learn anything of the hazards she might be expected to encounter.

Some Captains embarked on a camp without even knowing how to cook—one of these took the wise precaution of having all the food sent from home already cooked—but they learnt as they went along, and there is no record that anyone actually died from the effects.

There were some pioneers, however; who braved the dangers of camping under canvas in spite of the warnings of the wiseacres, and so blazed the trail for the thousands who now go every year to experience the joys of living in the open.

The first tented camp of which there is any record took place, oddly enough, in London, in the garden of the Commissioner for Hampstead. This was in 1910.

The following year Miss Agnes Maynard, known to her friends as The Carpenter, held her first camp at Whitstable. The Guides, seventy-five of them, came in relays from different parts of England and had a pretty strenuous time. One day they walked eighteen miles to have tea with the Canterbury Guides in their hall. Eight Guides learnt to row a boat alone, two learnt to swim, and one Patrol Leader cooked seven dinners and so gained her cook's badge.

It was quite usual for Miss Maynard's company to pile

Queen Alexandra arrives at post war rally in Hyde Park in 1918

all their kit on to a trek-cart and walk ten miles to the camp site, unloading and reloading several times on the way to get it over stiles and fences. If anyone questioned whether this was not too tiring for the girls, the Carpenter would tell them of the little Guide who rushed up to her immediately on arrival from such a trek and begged to be passed her skipping test there and then!

The First World War brought experiments in camping to an abrupt end, but no sooner was peace declared than renewed activity broke out, with a definitely military atmosphere pervading all Guides camps. In Scotland and Ulster an ex-sergeant seemed to be an indispensable member of the staff, and at one camp an army cook attended to pitch the tents, cook and serve the meals, which the campers then ate in the seclusion of their tents.

Often the Guides kept "sentry-go" all through the night, one watch relieving another every few hours. To sit in the glow of the camp fire on the look-out for "wild beasts" or "the enemy" while the rest of the camp slept was a real and never to be forgotten adventure.

Since the earliest days the Guides had been accused by their ill-wishers of being a military organization, and great efforts were constantly being made to show the public that this was not so. At about this time the word "officer" was replaced by "Guider", and the term was adopted throughout the Commonwealth, though the word "Leader" is more commonly used internationally.

As memories of the war grew dimmer, the military phase of Guiding, with its marching, drilling and heel-clicking, resolved itself into the artistic phase—or craze. Woodcraft became all the rage; trainers decorated their letters with drawings of bunnies in green ink; companies moved from place to place in Indian file, instead of marching in solid phalanxes, and it was rumoured that in Scotland campers strewed the grease pit each morning with freshly gathered wild flowers.

Whatever Guiding was doing, it was not standing still!

The Tree Grows Some Branches

It was not long before the Guides' younger sisters started to clamour for attention, as all younger sisters are apt to do. They could not see why they should have to wait for years and years until they were eleven to join in this lovely game. They started coming along to the meetings, and no doubt made themselves a bit of a nuisance, until at last, in 1914, the authorities were obliged to start a junior branch for these insistent youngsters.

I don't know who thought of calling them "Rosebuds", for most of them were far from flower-like, and the name did not stick. It was the Founder, with his genius for hitting on the right word, who re-christened them "Brownies", and suggested as a theme for their activities Mrs. Ewing's story of Tommy and Betty and the Brownies who did good turns in the home without ever being seen.

The Brownie, a mixture of good fairy and mischievous imp, is a well-known figure in the folk-lore of Great Britain, but he is not found everywhere, so, as Guiding started up in one country after another, a fascinating variety of names was adopted by different countries as being suitable for their youngest members.

Many small birds have been pressed into service, as for instance Greenfinches, Bul-buls, Bluebirds and Little Birds. Little Wings, applied to either birds or bees, are also found, as well as Ladybirds, Stars, Fairies and Gnomes of various kinds. One could go on almost for ever. You can find them in the series of World Association Brownie Painting Books if you are interested.

The stories for the various countries corresponding to Tommy and Betty and the Wise Brown Owl are naturally different too, but it would take a whole book to tell them all. The two fingers held up in the Brownie salute—or sign—was, however, universal for many years and so it figures on the World Brownie Badge introduced in 1955.

Cadets came on to the scene at much the same time as the Brownies, though sometimes they were so-called for no better reason than that they belonged to a school company. Soon, however, they were formed into a special section with a programme that included training as Guiders.

It was not until some years later that Senior Guides made their appearance. This was the inevitable result of girls enjoying Guiding so much that they did not want to give it up, even when they had grown too old for their companies and were blocking the way of the younger ones, who naturally became a bit bored with these "veterans"!

"Senior Guides" sounded rather dull, so everyone was asked to send in ideas for a new name to Headquarters and many fanciful suggestions arrived, including "Guideswomen" and "Eagerhearts".

It was the Founder again who thought of "Rangers". It is interesting to note that originally they were called "Ranger Guides", in line with "Rover Scouts". B.-P. said that the full name would explain what they were to the general public, while they could be known simply as "Rangers" within the movement. The second word, however, was lost in the course of time.

Guiding was originally taken up by girls who could "ride and swim and climb a tree and track a man", but children who could not do these things because they were ill and had to stay in bed were certainly not going to be left out.

There were several of these undaunted ones in a big

hospital at Carshalton. They read about Guides and they made up their minds that they, too, would be Guides.

All sorts of activities are possible even if your arms or legs are in plaster; that is, if you are determined not to be beaten. You can keep the Promise and Law lying down just as well as standing up—and that, after all, is what makes a real Guide.

The patients in St. Mary's Hospital started tying knots; hoisting flags on their bed-posts and signalling to one another down the ward. The Sister in charge naturally took an interest in these goings-on, and the girls persuaded her without much difficulty to teach them first aid. Then a curious thing happened. The doctors noticed that these patients were not only happier but that their health was actually improving, and so they suggested that as Guiding seemed to have such a good effect it ought to be extended.

That is how the girls of St. Mary's Hospital opened the door to "Extension Guides", as they are called. There are now many hundreds of companies and packs in hospitals, and in schools for the blind, the deaf and the physically and mentally handicapped. Those who live in their own homes, but are not strong enough to attend meetings, receive their training in the form of a letter through the post and are therefore "Post" Guides or Brownies. They are attached to local companies or packs whose members visit them as often as possible.

Handicapped Guides go to camp and do all the things that other Guides do. Some of the tests have had to be changed, but they are never made easier: indeed, these Guides pride themselves on the fact that in some things, such as handicrafts, their standard is higher. There is a depot at Headquarters where the things they make are

An Extension Guide learns to light a fire

sold, which you can see for yourself any day if you go there.

Extension Guiding has spread to many other countries. In France and Switzerland they are called Guides or Eclaireuses Malgré Tout—Guides in Spite of Everything—which is rather a good name, because in spite of their individual handicaps they are Guides—or Brownies or Rangers—just like all the rest.

Girls who live too far away from a company to go to meetings in the ordinary way may be "Lone Guides". They too, receive their training through the post, but there are not many in Great Britain nowadays, except in boarding schools where there may be no regular company. In countries of vast distances however, like Canada and South Africa, this is an important section.

In New Zealand and Australia the Lones have some of their "meetings" over the radio and are even enrolled "on the air".

Each member of the company answers to her name over the "transceiver" and then the Guider conducts the enrolment ceremony just as if everybody were assembled in the same place, the only difference being that after the girl has made her Promise her mother, instead of the Guider, pins on her Promise Badge.

Hands Across the Sea

Foundations

When he started this game for boys B.-P. had no idea, as we have seen, that it would appeal to girls; neither had he foreseen that it would spread far beyond the shores of his own country, and even of the British Commonwealth. It came as a complete surprise to him to find Scout groups popping up like mushrooms in places as far apart as Japan and Sweden, Brazil and Iceland.

Again it was not only the boys who took to Scouting; their sisters in most countries were just as enthusiastic.

By 1910 Guiding had begun in Canada, Denmark, South Africa and Finland; in 1911 it spread to India, The Netherlands and Sweden; in the next year or two more and more countries joined in.

These girls began scouting in exactly the same way as the girls in Great Britain. That is, by reading *Scouting for Boys* and borrowing their brothers' hats and their mothers' broomsticks.

It is very important to realise this, because so many people think that all other countries copied British Guiding; but as you can see by the dates given above this was not possible, for Guiding in Great Britain had hardly got going itself and was still in a fairly confused state, as regards organization and uniformity.

These other countries, then, took their ideas from the fountainhead—from B.-P. himself and the plan he had written down in *Scouting for Boys*, which had quickly been translated into many languages.

The British Guides who made the first trip abroad, to Hamburg in 1911

You may compare the growth of Guiding to the building of a house. The girls in each country laid the foundations—consisting of the Promise and Law, the Patrol System and the open air life—and then they built the walls and roof to fit in with their own geographical surroundings and their traditional way of life.

These "Guide Houses" are very much alike in some ways and very different in others, and that is what makes international Guiding so interesting.

Camping, so popular with Guides everywhere, provides many variations in technique. In Britain one never pitches a tent under trees for fear of the dangers that may arise from a storm suddenly blowing up, and it is still a challenge, though no longer a standard test, to light a fire in the open with two matches. In Cyprus, however, you must pitch your tent in the shade or risk being practically boiled alive, and you can set the whole neighbourhood ablaze with one match! To learn how to put out a fire seems more important than how to light one.

In some parts of Africa where people live a rather primitive life mostly in the open, the emphasis is on homecraft rather than on tracking and stalking, but the skills required are very different from those needed in a push-button all-electric home in an English city.

The first thrill on arriving at an international gathering is to see all the different uniforms and to guess—if you haven't done your homework very thoroughly beforehand—where they all come from, and maybe learn a little about the country, its climate and way of life simply from the uniform the girls are wearing.

Here is an Indian in traditional sari, and a Pakistani in salwar and khamiz—a loose blouse and trousers. The Americans are in green—their first uniform was navy like the early British, but it was impossible to keep it tidy during the dusty hot summer so sensibly they changed it. There is a girl in white—could she be from Mauritius? And others in grey or beige or brown.

But whatever their uniform, their camping or homecraft techniques they all try to live by the same code expressed in different languages.

The original Promise laid down by the Founder in *The Scheme for Girl Guides* was as follows:

I promise on my honour

      1)   To be loyal to God and the King

      2)   To try to do daily good turns

      3)   To obey the law of the Guides.

The wording, but not the sense, has been changed several times in the course of years, and in 1968 the same Threefold Promise was given to the Brownies instead of the Two-fold Promise they had made on enrolment up to that time—the same Promise, that is, except for the words 'Brownie Guide Law' instead of 'Guide Law'.

In some countries the Promise is made 'to my country' instead of to the king or queen; in some 'to my religion' or 'to the Church' instead of to God; a few include a promise 'to my family' and so the variations continue but the ideals are the same.

It may be mentioned here that Guiding is not confined to Christians, as it is sometimes thought, but includes members of all the great Faiths—Judaism, Islam, Buddhism, Hinduism and so on.

In several countries, Switzerland and France for example, a Guide may not necessarily make the Promise until she has been in the movement for quite a while, perhaps as long as two or three years. She may pass tests, win badges and go to camp, but making the Promise is considered to be so serious a responsibility that she is required to think deeply of the meaning of these few simple words, and not until she feels she really

understands what she is undertaking—for life—does she
go to her Leader and ask to be enrolled.

The Guide Promise
    I promise that I will do my best:
      To do my duty to God,
    To serve the Queen and help other people,
      and
    To keep the Guide Law

The Guide Law
1. A Guide is loyal and can be trusted.
2. A Guide is helpful.
3. A Guide is polite and considerate.
4. A Guide is friendly and a sister to all Guides.
5. A Guide is kind to animals and respects all living things.
6. A Guide is obedient.
7. A Guide has courage and is cheerful in all difficulties.
8. A Guide makes good use of her time.
9. A Guide takes care of her own possessions and those of other people.
10. A Guide is self-controlled in all she thinks, says and does.

The Brownie Guide Law
A Brownie thinks of others before herself and does a
Good Turn every day.

The Brownie Guide Motto
Lend a hand.

The Ranger Guide's Further Responsibility
To be of service to the community.

The above Guide Laws are much the same in all countries although the wording may be a little different, as in the following examples:

A Guide is a friend to animals and plants.

A Guide uses everything (i.e. tools, materials, etc.) in a proper manner.

A Guide has the team spirit.

A Guide bears disappointment with a smile.

After the World Association of Girl Guides and Girl Scouts came into being in 1928, all countries agreed to adopt the trefoil for their Promise Badge so that Guides everywhere might have this as the symbol of their common ideals.

Up to this time each group had used whatever design appealed to them, and sometimes there were several within a single country. You may imagine that it was not easy to give up a badge that had meant so much to the national pioneers, but they did it for the sake of unity in the world movement. In some of the existing badges the original symbol can be seen incorporated into a design with the trefoil.

It was not until 1949 that the World Badge, a golden trefoil on a bright blue background, was introduced to be worn by all Guides and Girl Scouts belonging to countries within the World Association, or to an International Company. It is sometimes used as the Promise Badge. In Great Britain it may be used in this way when a girl of foreign nationality is enrolled into a British company.

The World Flag—which is used in Great Britain as the Company Colour—also consists of a golden trefoil on a blue ground. It was at South Africa's suggestion that the World Conference of 1930 adopted this flag, which was designed by a Norwegian, so it has a true international history.

The three leaves of the trefoil—like the three fingers held up in the Guide sign—stand for the threefold Promise; the two stars signify the Promise and Law, in the centre is the compass needle pointing the right course; the base is the heraldic flame of love; while the colours are those of the sun in a clear sky which is above us all.

Olga Malkowska and the Polish Scouts

In many places Guiding started by girls getting together in patrols to practise scouting, but in two countries, both of which began it in 1912, the movement was founded by particular individuals.

Poland at this time was not an independent self-governing country; she was split up into three parts under the domination of Austria, Germany and Russia.

All young Poles dreamed of the day when Poland would be free and united; there were dozens of secret societies working for the day of liberation, but few of them had any plan for building up their country after that day dawned.

What appealed to Andrei Malkowski about Scouting was that not only would it help the boys and girls to prepare for the day of liberation, but it would also make them into useful citizens afterwards. Scouting could continue with as much zest and enthusiasm in a free Poland as under the existing regime.

He translated his copy of *Scouting for Boys* into Polish and asked a fellow student, Olga Drahonowska, to organize the girls.

Olga and Andrei lived in the Austrian zone where the authorities were less strict than in the other two; even so the Scouts and Guides usually met secretly. Often they would gather at 3 a.m. to start on a week-end hike, but this was more to cultivate strength of character than to evade the attentions of the police!

The Guides, who were mostly working girls of about fifteen, used to tell their mothers that they were going with a lady older than themselves, and that there would be some men to guard them. They did not think it necessary to explain that "the lady" was only eighteen and that "the men" were Boy Scouts, but Polish parents were so used to these mysterious secret societies that they did not worry overmuch.

In the summer of 1914 Andrei—who had in the meantime married Olga—decided to have a big camp in the Tatra mountains. They chose a site in a clearing of a huge forest and kept the whole project absolutely secret, except for telling their friend the local doctor.

Scouts and Guides were invited from the Russian and German zones, but since they were forbidden to travel they had to come under false names with forged passports, or else slip across the frontier under cover of the night. Scouting became a serious matter then.

There were all sorts of excitements in camp: the tent that caught fire; the spy who was caught in the Captain's tent trying to find out the real names of the children from across the frontiers; the bear that raided the larder; and the two cases of measles who were nursed back to health in the sick tent. Everybody had a good time, and then just before the camp was due to finish war was declared; the frontiers were closed, and the children from the other side were trapped, unable to go home.

Twice a victim of war, Olga Malkowska the founder of the Polish Guides Movement

Imagine the situation—300 boys and girls with nowhere to go! Andrei managed to find an empty house in the town for some of them, and billets for others; he stayed to see them settled in before he and the Rovers went off to join the Polish legion, leaving Olga and the other Leaders to look after the "colony".

The boys and girls had, of course, to earn their living. Every morning they paraded in the square and the jobs were given out. They started a tea-room in their house; helped the foresters with logging; took charge of the postal services when the professional staff went to fight; and ran a refugee centre for frightened people who had been driven from their homes.

Discipline was very strict. One dark wet night a girl who had been logging arrived home soaked through. She rubbed down her horse, fed him, and then came thankfully in to her own supper.

"Please give me the chit from the forester," said Olga. (This was the note that the forester filled in stating the number of hours worked, so that the correct pay could be drawn.)

"Oh dear!" said Lili, "I forgot to ask for it."

"In that case you will just have to go back and get it," said Olga.

"Yes, of course—so I will—tomorrow."

"The man will have forgotten by then. No my dear, you will have to go now, before he goes to bed."

"But you could not turn the horse out again on a night like this!" said the girl.

"I wasn't thinking of sending the horse," replied Olga. "It was not he who forgot the chit."

So Lili went out into the storm again, and she went cheerfully, realizing that it was no more than her duty.

As the boys grew old enough they joined the army, and the girls became nurses; bringing in the wounded from the battlefield was no longer a game but the deadly-earnest, heart-breaking business of life.

When Andrei and Olga planned their summer camp they had hardly foreseen that it would stretch on over several years.

Juliette Low—Recruiting Officer

"I do hate staying in hotels," said Daisy. "One has to get up so early in the morning."

"Good gracious, why?" asked her puzzled nephew.

"One is constantly reading in the newspapers of hotel robberies. If a burglar came into your room in the middle of the night, where do you suppose he would look for your jewellery?"

"On the dressing table, I suppose," said the nephew, "or else under the pillow."

"Exactly," said Daisy triumphantly. "So I always put my pearls in the toes of my shoes and put them outside the door. But then I have to get up and bring them in before the boot-boy takes them away."

You will see from this story that Daisy—or Mrs. Juliette Low—was an original thinker. She had logic, but not always the straightforward kind found in ordinary people.

Allied to this quality she had tremendous determination and great charm of manner. She knew what she wanted, and she could nearly always persuade people to take on jobs they had absolutely no intention of doing when she first approached them. Usually the jobs were well done, too, for Daisy selected her victims with care.

Owing to an accident in her youth she was almost stone deaf, but she turned this handicap to advantage by literally not hearing the objections urged against any scheme she had in mind.

She was born in Savannah, Georgia, of American

parents, but lived all her married life in England. Soon after she was left a widow she met B.-P., and from that moment she knew what she wanted—to bring Guiding to the girls of her own country.

Juliette Low at Foxlease

She had taken a house in Scotland that summer of 1911, and had invited some young army officers to stay for the shooting—but they were lucky if ever they saw a grouse! Daisy had started a Guide company among the daughters of the crofters, and the young men spent their time creeping through the heather, signalling and mapping with her girls.

Returning to London she started two more companies—one of them in Lambeth—which she ran for a couple of months, and then, as she was leaving England for the United States, she looked for a victim to take her place.

She sent for a young woman of her acquaintance, explained about the company in Lambeth and finished, "As I am sailing on Wednesday I have told the girls that you will go down on Thursday and look after them till I get back."

According to her usual habit Daisy turned a deaf ear to all the excellent reasons why her friend could not do as she commanded and said simply, "Splendid—I knew I could count on you!" and was gone! The victim had no intention of being victimized—but when Thursday came she thought of those poor girls waiting for her—and she went down to Lambeth.

Daisy's shrewd judgment had not deserted her, for this new recruit to Guiding was Mrs. Mark Kerr, of whom we shall hear much more.

Enter the Chief Guide

When Mrs. Low sailed for the United States that famous Wednesday in January 1912, she boarded the S.S. *Arcadian*, and found among her fellow passengers Baden-Powell himself, off on a world tour of Scouting, and also a dutiful daughter accompanying her father on a cruise for his health. We caught a glimpse of this young woman some time ago, buying a souvenir button of her soldier hero.

It was purely by chance that Mr. Soames had booked a passage in the same ship as the Chief Scout, but it turned out a lucky chance for the Guides.

"The only interesting person on board," Olave wrote to her mother at the outset of the voyage, "is the Scout man."

Lord and Lady Baden-Powell unveiling 'The Girl Guide', Euston in 1931

He interested her from the very beginning by saying, "Do you often exercise your dog in Hyde Park?"

"Why, no," she replied. "I don't live in London."

"But you have got a brown and white spaniel," he persisted, "and I saw you out with him one day last year near Knightsbridge barracks."

B.-P. was quite right. Olave had been on a visit to London at that time. He had only seen her back, but he had noticed her walk and had recognized it as soon as she boarded the ship.

They discovered another coincidence. They shared a birthday—February 22nd—although B.-P. had been born thirty-two years before Olave.

Before the Chief Scout left the ship at Jamaica they were engaged—unofficially—and were married when he returned from his tour in·October, 1912. B.-P. could not have chosen a better person to be World Chief Guide!

Meanwhile Mrs. Low went .on to her home town, Savannah. There she at once collected together all the girls she could lay hands on, told them about Guiding and before the evening was out the first company of Girl Guides in the United States was well on its way.

"We can use the stable back of the house for meetings, and my empty lot across the way for games, and before I go away I will get you a good leader." So said Mrs. Low and was as good as her word. That very evening she rang up a friend and said, "Come right over. I have something here for the girls of Savannah, and all America, and all the world. And we're going to begin it tonight."

On leaving Savannah, Mrs. Low toured America. In each place she collected a group of girls, inspired them with enthusiasm to become Guides and then, using her charm and her deafness, procured them a grown-up Leader.

That is how the Girl Guides—later re-named the Girl Scouts—started in the United States. There are now over three million of them, all due to an indomitable little woman who wouldn't take 'NO' for an answer.

The Chief Guide Goes Fishing

The first world war might well have brought the Scout and Guide Movement to an end—it was, after all, only six years old, and the girls' side of it, even in Great Britain, was far from being completely organized.

Miss Baden-Powell and her Headquarters Committee, however, worked on steadily in spite of war-time difficulties, and after a time Lady Baden-Powell, who had been helping in the Boy Scout and Y.M.C.A. Rest Hut at Calais, came to join the team.

In 1916 a conference was held at Swanwick in Derbyshire. "Commissioners" had only recently been invented, and there were not nearly as many as were needed. Lady Baden-Powell worked hard at that conference. She went around with a map writing in the names of the people she managed to persuade to take on the job of County Commissioner.

It was the time when "bobbing" had just come into fashion and Lady B.-P. was longing to have her hair cut short, but the Chief Scout said he would only allow it when every county was equipped with a commissioner. "That sounds rather like 'never'," she said sadly looking at the blank spaces on her map. In the end, however, it only took a year or two, but she never cut off her hair after all.

The immediate result of her hard work was that at the end of the conference she was appointed Chief Commissioner—a position she held until 1925. In 1918 she was given the title of Chief Guide.

In spite of the labours of the grown-ups, in the intervals of war-work, the movement would never have survived, either in Great Britain or elsewhere, had it not been for the splendid spirit and determination of the children.

The seed of Scouting which the Founder had planted had struck deeper roots than most people imagined, and although a great number of troops and companies were left without grown-up leadership in 1914, the girls and boys realized that this was an opportunity to prove themselves—and prove themselves they did.

In the countries directly involved in the bitter fighting many Scouts and Guides showed extraordinary courage and devotion to duty, while in those luckier countries, which were not actually invaded, unspectacular work was undertaken and regularly and faithfully performed.

So the movement weathered the storm of 1914-1918, and was even found to be more firmly established than ever when peace was at last declared.

The Chief Guide was never one to let the grass grow under her feet. The war was barely over when she set out to get all the information she could about Guides in other countries.

She knew the movement was going ahead in the Commonwealth and, through Mrs. Low, that the American Girl Scouts were making great strides, but of other countries there was little news and it was often not even known if Guiding had survived.

Something must be done to find out, thought Lady B.-P., and so she formed the International Council which met for the first time in February 1919. She herself was chairman, and as her vice-chairman she chose Rose Kerr.

Mrs. Kerr had not been idle since she had been trapped by Mrs. Low. She had given up her original company on going to live in Greece in 1913, but soon after she came back to England, in 1916, she was invited to spend a week-end with the Baden-Powells. She little knew that she was to be "victimized" once again!

Mrs Mark Kerr

All unsuspecting she went down—she was an old friend of the Founder's—to see the babies and to talk about her travels. Nothing was said about Guiding until the last morning; then while she was quietly having her bath she heard the Chief Guide banging on the door and calling out, "Rosie, you must be Commissioner for London—do say yes!"

"Wait at least till I have dried myself," she replied,

and presently emerged to make the usual excuses—lack of time and talent—but her attempt at refusal was brushed aside, and thinking perhaps that she might get no breakfast if she held out, she at last assented. She remained County Commissioner for London until 1941.

Lady B.-P. did not know it at the time, but in fact she had landed much more than a County Commissioner, so you may say she had a very good morning's fishing in the bath.

The First International Get-Together

When Mrs. Kerr was asked to become vice-chairman of the International Council she was long past the stage of excuses. She was right in the movement, as keen as she could be, and this new job particularly appealed to her. She had been educated in France and Germany, spoke six languages fluently (with a smattering of as many more) and had friends scattered all over the world with whom she was in close touch, for she was a great letter-writer.

The members of the Council were all people who lived in England but who had some connection or another with a foreign country; such as a Belgian married to an Englishman, or a diplomat's wife who had been *en poste* in the Argentine. The duty of each member was to write to the people she knew in "her" country and find out if there were any Guides there, and if so what they were doing.

The International Council was really a clearing-house for information; it never tried to "teach" the Guides in other lands, but it gave advice if it were asked.

It was all very unofficial and amateurish—but how exciting! News came in of large numbers of Guides in some places, and then of little struggling groups in others; at every meeting a new space was filled in on the map of the world, till it seemed that there were Guides almost everywhere, even if in some regions they were spread rather thin.

Then one day the Chief Guide—always full of good ideas—said, "Let's ask two or three Guiders from each of these countries to come over here so that we can get to know each other!"

It was the first time an international gathering had been contemplated and everyone was enthusiastic, so the invitations were sent out.

As the time drew near for this historic conference, the British County Commissioners, who had been asked to come too, wondered more and more what their guests would be like.

"Will they wear uniform?" they asked each other.

"Navy blue like us or something different?"

"What language shall we speak?"

"Will they have the right idea of Guiding?"

"Will they (horrid thought) think us very queer?"

You see, hardly any of them had ever seen a foreign Guide before.

All these questions, and many more, were answered at St. Hugh's College, Oxford, in July, 1920, when what is now known as the First International Conference took place.

It was a tremendous success. The "foreigners" were no longer thought of as "foreigners" but as sister Guides, and such they remained for ever afterwards.

The principal thing of interest to Guides of to-day was that the Americans introduced 'Taps' to the movement:

Day is gone;
Gone the sun;
From the hills, from the sea, from the sky.
All is well; safely rest;
God is nigh.

It is not certain why this evening bugle call is named
Taps; but it may be connected with the tapping of the
drum which recalled soldiers to camp at nightfall.
Whatever the origin, it was taken up with enthusiasm
and sung by Guides all over the world to close their
meetings, regardless of whether the day was ending or
not, until some "daylight" words were produced for
occasions when the sun was shining.

A House of Our Own

Just imagine that you are a Guide who is going to be
presented to the Queen at a big rally. What preparations
you would make!

You would see that your uniform was spotlessly
clean, press your skirt, polish your shoes and badges;
then you would have an extra special wash and brush up
and altogether make sure that you were as neat as a new
pin, because everybody, from the Queen down, would
be looking at you.

If you were just going out to do something quite
ordinary you might not take so much trouble, and yet
you never know who might not look at you and
say—what?

I am sure the Bournemouth Guides who went to
camp in an empty house in the summer of 1921 had no
idea that they were about to make history just because
somebody was impressed by them.

The house they were lent was a lovely place in the

New Forest in Hampshire. It belonged to an American, Mrs. Archbold, and it was called Foxlease.

Mrs. Archbold had gone back to live in the United States, and she had told her Agent to give the house to any society that was doing good work and would like to have it.

The house had been empty for some time when the Guides arrived for their indoor camp, and as is the way with houses that are left empty, even the nicest ones, it had collected a certain amount of dust and dirt.

The Guides set to work at once. They scrubbed the floors—there were a lot of rooms, too—polished the door-handles and washed the paint.

One day the Agent came to call. He walked through all the rooms and saw the shining brass and spotless boards and was evidently very much impressed by the cared-for appearance of the place, because he said to the Commissioner in Charge, "I believe you have given me an idea. Do you know if the Girl Guides want a house?"

The Commissioner replied, "As a matter of fact I happen to know that they DO. Several people have been saying lately, 'If only we had a place of our own for training and conferences, how wonderful it would be.' You had better talk to the Chief Guide about it." The Agent went away and did that very thing.

Lady Baden-Powell could hardly believe her ears when this breath-taking offer was made to her. A beautiful, historic old house in a perfect position, with lovely grounds for camping, seemed too good to be true!

But there was one snag. The property would cost a lot of money to keep up; there would be rates and repairs as well as the expense of furnishing and equipping it. Could the Association possibly afford it?

While the decision hung in the balance the Chief Guide was struck down by 'flu'; but as she lay in bed feeling very ill indeed a wonderful thing happened.

Mrs. Mark Kerr had a telephone call:

"This is Lady Mary Trefusis, Lady-in-Waiting to Princess Mary," said the voice at the other end of the line. "Her Royal Highness has received a very large sum of money as a wedding present from the 'Marys' of the Commonwealth. The Committee dealing with this money would like to suggest spending some of it in presenting a house as a training centre to the Girl Guides, since Her Royal Highness is their President. Would they care to accept such a gift?"

Mrs. Kerr was hopping with excitement. She explained that they had already been offered a house, but that it needed equipping and furnishing. Could not the money be used in this way?

Lady Mary did not think that would be at all the same thing; they would like to give the actual house and name it after the Princess. A decision must be made at once as the 'Marys' were presenting their gift the following day and wished to lay a definite scheme before Her Royal Highness.

"In that case you had better telephone Lady Baden-Powell," said Mrs. Kerr.

So Lady Mary rang up the Chief Guide, who suggested that, if Foxlease were endowed by Her Royal Highness, it could be named "Princess Mary House" and so connect her forever with this much-desired Guide centre.

When the Chief Guide put down the receiver she found that the excitement had quite cured her of the 'flu! She jumped out of bed, dressed and went straight up to London to consult various people. Next day she called at Buckingham Palace; cabled Mrs. Archbold in America; received an answer; and finally the whole thing was settled.

Princess Mary, later the Princess Royal and President of the Girl Guides, at Foxlease

In the end Princess Mary not only gave £6,000 from the 'Marys' gift but also £4,000 from the money taken at the exhibition of her wedding presents.

Princess Mary—later The Princess Royal—had first become interested in Guides when a company, which she often used to visit, was started at Sandringham in Norfolk. In 1920 she became president of the Girl Guides Association, and Miss Baden-Powell, who had held this position previously, became Vice-President.

The Princess was never a mere figurehead, but took part in countless rallies and conferences and altogether proved one of the most ardent friends of the movement. The Guides can never be grateful enough to her for making it possible for them to accept Mrs. Archbold's magnificent present—but let them also remember the Bournemouth Guides who started the ball rolling!

Guides from all over the Commonwealth and even from other countries adopted rooms at Foxlease and furnished them, so that problem was quickly solved. The two cottages were claimed by the United States and Canada, and Mrs. Low hurried down to the one named "The Link" (between Great Britain and U.S.A.) to oversee personally the fixing of a bath and to paint the furniture. Scotland chose—appropriately—the lovely drawing-room, which is a fine example of the work of the famous eighteenth century architects and decorators, Robert and John Adam, themselves Scots. In no time at all it seemed the house was ready to receive its first guests.

It is nice to think that shortly after it was opened in 1922, twenty-two delegates from the Second International Conference held at Newnham College, Cambridge, went straight on to Foxlease and took part in almost the first training ever held there.

Foxlease was such a success that in 1927 Waddow Hall, on the borders of Lancashire and Yorkshire, was brought to serve as a training centre for the North of England. Scotland, Wales and Ulster opened their centres shortly after the end of the Second World War. They are called Netherurd, Broneirion and Lorne, respectively, and all stand in equally lovely surroundings, offering a welcome to visitors from all over the world as well as to the Guiders of their own countries.

One World

The First World Camp

Picture to yourself a beautiful old French Château set amongst the woods and orchards of Normandy. "Just the perfect place for a camp!" you might think; and so it was!

A company of Guides from Belgium, another from France and a third from England came together in 1922 in the grounds of the Château d'Argeronne for the very first real international camp, the fore-runner of many others.

The camp chores were undertaken by each country in turn, and nobody who was there will ever forget the Belgians' cooking. It did not seem possible that such exquisite meals could be conjured up over an open fire!

The campers might have grown very fat as a result but luckily the French were rather Spartan, and organized the most exciting wide games in the woods which hardly allowed time to eat at all—while the English were chiefly notable for the hard work they put into cleaning dixies!

Was the Chief Guide perhaps thinking of this camp as she walked through the stubble fields near her home in Hampshire the following summer?

The evening sun shone down on the peaceful English countryside; the children, Peter, Heather and Betty trotted ahead on their ponies while their parents strolled along chatting to their friend Olivia Burges.

Suddenly the Chief Guide said, "What about a WORLD camp?"

The idea was so terrific that the three of them stopped dead in their tracks. Then they sat down on a corn-stook and worked out the whole thing on the spot.

The Baden-Powell family

It would be held at Foxlease at the same time as the Third International Conference; the Chief Guide would invite all countries to send six Guides and one Guider; Olivia would be secretary . . .

It was not surprising that they were late home for supper.

In the summer of 1924 Foxlease presented an

animated scene. Hundreds of tents dotted the green expanse of grass and girls' voices, speaking a dozen or more languages, echoed through the Forest.

Five hundred British Patrol Leaders acted as hostesses to their six hundred guests from other countries.

They were divided up into thirty group camps, each one equipped and staffed by a different country.

In these small groups, about the size of a company camp, the Guides were nicely mixed up in Patrols.

There is no better way of getting to know people than by working with them; and camp chores—or capers as the Americans call them—are certainly fine things for breaking down barriers. Nobody remembers to feel shy when the stew is in danger of falling into the fire, and a lack of German or French or Japanese does not seem to matter when you are struggling to make those complicated rolls of hessian and poles transform themselves into a neat row of wash cubicles.

So it was at the first world camp—everybody made friends in the shortest possible time.

There was only one worried person and that was the Blanket-Sorter.

A great many of the visitors arrived unprepared to face the rigours of an English summer. It was, of course, pouring with rain and bitterly cold, so the quartermaster telegraphed to London for 200 extra blankets. They were to be sent down at once, and the transport people met every train all through the day. Ten o'clock came and with it the last train from London, but no blankets. It was still raining. Something had to be done if the guests from warmer climes were to get a wink of sleep that night.

Late as it was the drivers set out to comb the

countryside for blankets. The neighbours rose magnificently to the occasion: hotels, private families and an army camp, all came to the rescue and around midnight the triumphant staff returned and distributed their spoils.

Next day the missing blankets arrived, but the borrowed ones had to be run to earth, sorted and returned to their (probable) rightful owners. The hastily appointed Blanket-Sorter spent the rest of the camp on the job!

After the first day the rain stopped and the sun shone for the remainder of that marvellous week.

Every night campers and delegates to the conference sat together round a glowing camp-fire and joined in the songs from many lands.

There beneath the stars with the sparks flying upwards they felt truly like one united family.

The World Visits the United States

Three International Conferences had now been held in England, and everybody thought that the next one should take place in another country, so Rosie Kerr went over to Switzerland to discuss the possibility of its being held there, but when she returned to England Mrs. Low sent for her and was perfectly furious.

"Of course the conference must take place in America," she said, "since we have always wanted it!"

"That would be very nice, I am sure," said Mrs. Kerr, "but it would be very expensive for the European countries to send delegates across the Atlantic and I don't think many of them could afford it. None of the Guide Associations has much money you know."

"That does not matter," declared Mrs. Low, drawing

on her imagination as usual, "because the United States will pay all expenses for one delegate from every country."

It was no use trying to cross Daisy when once she had made up her mind, so that was that.

A few days later she sailed for America to make her decision known to the Girl Scouts' National Board!

The Director of the Board loved to tell how she received a telegram saying "Meet me in Boston. I have a plan."

Knowing Mrs. Low she let her imagination play with all sorts of wild ideas, but she never approached the colossal scheme which Daisy laid before her when she arrived, in a kind of whirlwind, at the rendezvous.

There was not only to be a conference for the grown-ups. "The girls can come, too," she said. "I talked it all over with the Captain of the ship coming across, and he can see no objection. They will come only as visitors so there will be no trouble with the immigration authorities. Then, of course, they must see something of the States while they are here. I have drawn up plans for one or two tours which will take them to a number of interesting and beautiful places. And I want the conference and camp to be located at Camp Edith Macy."

Daisy's listener was speechless. The whole thing seemed quite impossible . . . and yet she could not help being carried along on a wave of enthusiasm. She saw the whole grand project through Daisy's eyes, and the fact that Camp Edith Macy (which had only just been presented to the Girl Scouts) was still only an untrodden hillside without even a road leading to it, seemed, after all, only a minor obstacle.

A few days later the scheme was laid before the
Executive Committee. To say that they were staggered
would be to put it mildly. But again, as Mrs. Low
talked, they were carried along with her. Yes, it was a
splendid plan, but not for the following year, they must
have time to make all the arrangements. They suggested
that 1928 would be quite soon enough.

Daisy, however, could not agree. "Now is the time,"
she said. "We need not have the girls over, if that is
asking too much, or the tours; just the conference . . .
but it must be next year. If it is any later I shall not be
there."

Then they realized suddenly that in spite of her
energy, her enthusiasm, her determination, Mrs. Low
was a sick woman.

When the project was put to the vote all were
unanimous that the 4th International Conference should
be held at Camp Edith Macy in May, 1926.

At once a real American hustle got going.

A road was built, wells were sunk; water-pipes were
laid; the splendid "Great Hall" was constructed as the
centrepiece. At times it seemed that Macy would never
be ready, but finally, as the last workmen were seen out
of the back door, the delegates were welcomed at the
front.

Mrs. Low was greeted first of all by American
Commissioners from almost every State, then she turned
round and, becoming one of them, welcomed the Chief
Guide and the representatives from twenty-nine
countries.

The foreign delegates had arrived in New York a few
days earlier; few of them had ever visited the United
States before and they were quite unprepared for the

stupendous reception that had been prepared for them, not only by the Girl Scouts, but by the Civil Authorities as well.

In their own countries, although the Guides were generally approved, they were not as a rule treated with great pomp and circumstance, and it came as a pleasing surprise to be made to feel immensely important.

They were met on board the Olympic by members of the National Board of the Girl Scouts and a delegation from the Manhattan Council. Then they were driven to Girl Scout Headquarters, and what a drive it was! The streets were cleared of traffic for the long procession of cars; speed-cops on motor cycles roared ahead of them and behind them, while crowds of people stopped to stare.

So it went on all day, until one delegate said wistfully: "How shall I go out when I get home with no policemen to escort me?" While another remarked nervously: "I think something must have gone wrong. I have not seen a movie-camera directed at me for at least ten minutes."

In the evening the party embarked on the S.S. New York bound for Boston, where once more they were fêted as honoured guests. On they went to Washington, the seat of the United States Government, where again they enjoyed the lavish hospitality so typical of America; then back to New York they travelled and so finally to Camp Edith Macy.

The tour planned by Mrs. Low did after all take place, and continued after the conference was over to Buffalo and Niagara and then on into Canada.

It was the supreme moment in Mrs. Low's life to see in her own homeland this great gathering of friends,

representing the world of Guiding. Fourteen years
before in Savannah she had said, "I have something here
for the girls . . . of all the world," and she had proved
right; Guiding was spreading rapidly, as could easily be
seen by looking around this assembly, for gathered
together were Leaders from Africa, Asia, Europe, North
and South America.

It had been her dream to have an international
conference in her own country, and her dream had
come true.

But her prophecy also came true: she died in January
1927. She was buried in Savannah, with the Girl Scouts
she loved forming a Guard of Honour. The flag on the
City Hall flew at half mast to mark the townspeople's
sorrow at her passing; and with her was buried a
telegram she had received from the National Board a
few days before:

"You are not only the first Girl Scout, but the best
Girl Scout of them all".

Mrs. Low worked not only for the girls of her own
country, but for girls everywhere, and her memory is
kept green by the fund raised in her honour by her
friends.

The Juliette Low World Friendship Fund is devoted
to the work that was most near to her heart:
international understanding between girls of all nations;
and many a girl born long after her death and living
thousands of miles from Savannah has cause to bless the
name of Juliette Low—Founder of the Girl Scouts of
the United States.

The World Association is Born

The 4th International Conference proved to be a

landmark in Guiding, for it was here that the seed was sown that grew into the great tree, with many branches spreading far and wide, which we call The World Association of Girl Guides and Girl Scouts.

The idea of setting up this World Association, to take the place of the informal International Council, was mentioned in conversation at the conference, but it was not until later that the European delegates, travelling home together across the Atlantic, discussed the plan in detail and came to a definite conclusion.

They chose two of their number to go to the Founder as soon as he got back to England (he and the Chief Guide were touring in America) and tell him that they thought the time had come for a World Association to be formed, in which the countries practising Guiding or Girl Scouting would be represented officially.

There were several reasons for this.

Guiding and Scouting had become so popular that often groups would spring up who called themselves Guides or Girl Scouts, but who were really not Guides at all, because they did not have the same ideals, although they might go camping and carry on similar activities.

You can easily imagine this happening; but in a country with a proper Guide Association a company is registered at Headquarters and then everybody knows that the members are true Guides who believe in the Promise and Law and try to obey the rules which are made by the Association.

If there were a World Association, said the delegates, the countries who were members of it would be known to be carrying on Guiding in the way that Sir Robert Baden-Powell had suggested.

Then again a group in a "new" country might want to be real Guides, but would not know where to turn for help. The World Association would be there to give advice and send a trainer, to make sure that they learnt to play the game in the right way.

The Founder listened sympathetically to all that was said on the subject of a World Association. The Boy Scouts had recently formed their own international organization, and he well understood the need, so he wrote a letter to all countries asking them to think the matter over very carefully and bring their views to the next International Conference which was due to take place in Hungary in 1928.

Meanwhile he asked Dame Katharine Furse to work out a detailed plan of how this proposed World Association might be organized; what its duties might be and what responsibilities the member countries should undertake. Another important question was where the money would come from to run it, as there would obviously have to be an office and some full-time secretaries to deal with all the correspondence which was sure to follow.

All these problems Dame Katharine was to consider, bringing her findings to the next conference, so that the delegates from the different countries could get an idea of how the scheme might be carried out. Of course, nothing Dame Katharine proposed would be adopted without full discussion by the delegates, who could suggest any alterations they thought advisable. After that, all these suggestions would have to be taken back to the various countries for discussion, and the final decisions brought to the conference to be held in 1930.

It sounds, doesn't it, as if it called for a lot of hard work and hard thinking?

Dame Katharine has been called the Architect of the World Association because of the great part she played in its formation, and also because she became the first Director of the World Bureau, which is what the headquarters of the World Association is called.

Who was this woman in whom so much trust was placed?

She was the daughter of the famous writer, John Addington Symonds, and although English by birth had been brought up in Switzerland where she met and married the artist, Charles Furse. He painted a picture of her as a girl holding two greyhounds; you may have seen reproductions of it. It is called "Diana of the Uplands", and the original now hangs in the Tate Gallery in London.

Charles Furse died after only a few years of marriage and Katharine threw all her great ability and intelligence into work for other people. She became head of the British Red Cross Society, and in the 1914-18 war she started and directed the Women's Royal Naval Service.

When the war came to an end she was very tired and needed a rest, but the Chief Guide had her eye on her, and was determined to bring her into the Guide movement.

Lady B.-P. was a good "fisherwoman", as we saw earlier in this story, and she finally hooked and landed Dame Katharine, but it took her longer than one morning! The Chief Guide enrolled Katharine on April 28th, 1922, and recorded in her diary that night, with a justifiable air of triumph: "She is in at last!" After that "Dame K." quickly made her mark on the movement.

She was one of those people who are always questioning, searching, seeking to improve.

Mrs. Kerr declared that her motto was evidently the same as that written up in the great Ford Motor Works: "There is nothing we are doing that could not be better done, and we must never cease to strive for this."

Dame K. was certainly not one to rest on her laurels, nor did she ever allow anybody else to rest on theirs!

She began her Guide career as Assistant Chief Commissioner to Lady Baden-Powell, who said that this showed her greatness of character. She had been the head of two very big and important services, but now she was content to take second place to a woman much younger and less experienced in administration than herself.

Dame K. also became head of the recently started section called Sea Guides later renamed Sea Rangers and many former officers in the W.R.N.S. followed their Chief into Guiding.

But Dame Katharine was destined for a much wider sphere of activity. It is interesting to learn that the delegates from the 4th International Conference, who planned the World Association on that famous trip across the Atlantic, had already decided that she and no other was the person for the job of Director of the World Bureau (if they ever had one), while quite independently B.-P. had picked her for the same position.

Parad is a little town in Hungary. It was lily-of-the-valley time when the delegates to the 5th International Conference assembled there and the sweet scent of the flowers, which carpeted the ground, filled all the air with fragrance.

Not wishing to be outdone by the splendid American reception of the previous occasion, the Hungarian Girl

Scouts had planned a wonderful week of festivities in Budapest before the conference opened.

Hungary is famous for its horses and an expedition was made to see some of them at home on their native plains. The Secretary of the International Council aroused great admiration by mounting one of them and galloping away into the distance, returning at last, to the relief of her companions, still secure in the saddle, which, according to the local custom, had no girths.

It would be untrue to say that this epoch-making conference ran on oiled wheels.

Many of the delegates were pioneers of Guiding in their own countries. They were women of strong character and determination, qualities of which they had had need in the early days. They expressed their views forcibly, and their views often differed. They were not at that time accustomed to working internationally.

It must be remembered, too, that the war had only ended ten years before, and that since then several neighbouring European countries had achieved self-government for the first time for many years. Hungary was one of them, Poland and Czechoslovakia others while Austria's great empire had been pruned away leaving only a tiny country no bigger than the rest. Rivalries between these Central European countries were very strong, each one wishing to show the world her national tradition and splendour.

It was all very natural, but it led to difficulties. It is so easy to say, "We shall all join together in one united sisterhood," but when it comes to practical details it is another matter. So it was at Parad.

In several countries there were two or more Guide associations. One, for instance, might be confined to

Roman Catholics, as in France and Belgium, or to members of the Y.W.C.A., as in Denmark, Sweden and Norway, whilst another might be open to any girl. Since it was proposed that recognition should be given only to the country as a whole it meant that these rival Associations would have to co-operate by forming a joint Council to represent them at world level.

There was also the question of the Promise badge, mentioned previously, and a number of similar problems.

Every country therefore had to make sacrifices—and it is always one's own sacrifice that seems harder than anybody else's!—and everyone had to pay.

It was a great triumph for the Guide spirit when the newer countries at last agreed to sink their differences and work together for the good of children everywhere in the world. It was also a great tribute to the patience and understanding of the people from the older countries.

The outcome of the Conference was that a World Committee of nine outstanding Leaders, with Mrs. Mark Kerr as Chairman, was elected to carry on the work until the next Conference; the World Bureau was set up with Dame Katharine Furse as Director; and *The Council Fire,* which had already been in existence for three years, was named as the official journal of World Guiding.

All these points, and many others, being settled, the International Council, which had done the pioneer work in bringing together the Guides of the world, met for the last time, and having officially "wound itself up"—as the Chief Guide put it—made way for its daughter: The World Association of Girl Guides and Girl Scouts.

Our Chalet

There must be a special Good Fairy attending to the wishes of the Guide Movement. In 1922 she heard somebody say "If only we had a house of our own . . ." and lo and behold there was Foxlease!

A few years later somebody said once again, "If only we had a house of our own . . ." but this time the wish was for a World Guide House where girls from all countries could come and feel it was their very own home.

No sooner were the words uttered, it seemed, than another Fairy Godmother appeared and said, "I should like to give that house!"

This Fairy Godmother came from Boston, Massachusetts, and her name was Mrs. James Storrow, but most people called her Aunt Helen.

The first time Sir Robert and Lady Baden-Powell visited the United States together, Mrs. Low said they must meet Aunt Helen, because she was one of the most important people in Girl Scouting.

Aunt Helen was not particularly keen about this meeting at the time.

"I suppose," she thought, "they are coming here to tell us how to do Scouting, but we know what we want for our girls and there is no need for them to come butting in with their British ideas." She may have said as much to Mrs. Low, and no doubt Mrs. Low turned her deaf ear!

Anyway, the Baden-Powells came to see Mrs. Storrow in her home near Boston with no idea that they were about to meet any hostility.

They walked into the room; Mrs. Storrow looked at them . . . at the man with a twinkle in his blue eyes and at his young dark-haired wife . . . and she surrendered at once to their charm.

By the end of the afternoon "Sir Robert"—which sounded like "Sir Rabbit" in her strong American accent—had become "Brer Rabbit", and Brer Rabbit she called him ever afterwards. In later years the three of them often used to laugh together over Aunt Helen's misgivings before that first meeting.

In 1929 Mrs. Storrow succeeded Mrs. Mark Kerr as Chairman of the World Committee, so she was in a good position to know the needs of the new young World Association; and since she was as rich as she was generous she said, "I should like to give that house, and I should like it to be in Switzerland."

Almost before anyone had time to draw breath she had whisked Dame Katharine off to Switzerland to start house-hunting. She enlisted the help of the Chief Scout of Switzerland and of a Swiss Guider called Ida von Herrenschwand, later to be known to generations of Guides as "Falk"—for she eventually became the first Guider-in-charge of the Guide House for which they were now searching.

As they set out Dame Katharine warned Falk, "If you feel hungry at any time please say so, for otherwise Mrs. Storrow will not stop for so trifling a matter as a meal."

Up hill and down dale they trudged, but the perfect house eluded them. Aunt Helen was undismayed. "If we cannot find a house ready-made," she said, "we can build one. All we have to do is to find the right place." But even that seemed difficult.

Then one day they came to a very beautiful spot overlooking a lake. Aunt Helen was enchanted. She climbed up on to the rocks, which lay here and there, to take photographs from every possible angle and grew quite ecstatic over the view.

"Here," she said, "is 'The Place'! Here one can find peace for the soul."

Falk remained silent. Certainly the place was very lovely, but she thought it was a bit tame.

"When I was sixteen," she was thinking, "which is the age of the girls who will come to our house, I was more interested in ski-ing and mountain climbing than in peace for the soul."

The 1930 World Conference was to be held soon at Foxlease, and Mrs. Storrow insisted that Falk must come to it and give her views.

"Please don't ask me to do that," said Falk. "You know we disagree about this place, and after all you are giving the chalet, not I."

Mrs. Storrow, however, still insisted. "And when you are asked for your opinion," she went on, "you jolly well say what you think!"

So Falk came to Foxlease. She spent a sleepless night before the day on which the proposed chalet was to be discussed. How could she possibly tell this formidable array of V.I.P's that she did not like the place on which the generous donor had set her heart?

The ordeal proved just as bad as she had anticipated. The delegates looked at Aunt Helen's photographs—how lovely they were!—and Falk could feel their disapproval as she herself explained about the "peace of her soul".

She felt miserable—and then she saw B.-P. grinning at her.

"Well, Falk," he said, "if you don't think this place suitable you will just have to go and find another one!"

Oh the relief of that moment! But what about kind

Aunt Helen? She would surely be upset at this decision.
But Mrs. Storrow seemed quite content that the search
should begin all over again, even though she herself
would not be able to take part in it as she had to return
to the United States.

Our Chalet

One day some weeks later Falk rushed into Guide
Headquarters in Berne crying, "I have found 'The
Place'!"

She expected everyone to leap up in excitement, but
they all went calmly on with their work. It seemed that
it was at least the twentieth time she had found the
perfect place. But this time it turned out to be true as
you may see for yourself if you go there.

Our Chalet—Nôtre Chalet—Unser Chalet—according to the language you speak—stands across the valley from Adelboden with mountain peaks rising all around it: the Wildstrubel, the Lohner, the Bonder, the Elsighorn—names now known and loved by thousands of Guides and Girl Scouts.

A few weeks before the opening, in July 1932, Mrs. Storrow came to see if all were in readiness. She found Falk and her team of helpers struggling to get the place in order. Gifts of equipment and furniture had come from all over the world, and everyone was up to the eyes in work, unpacking, sorting and putting everything in the appropriate place; moreover, they were expecting a thousand or more guests for the ceremonial opening, and cakes had to be ordered and arrangements made. Nobody could imagine what would happen if it rained; the house was built to accommodate sixty, where would one put one thousand—maybe two thousand—visitors? The weather during these weeks was not promising and everyone was getting more and more nervous, so Falk issued an order, "Nobody is to mention, or even think, about the weather."

In the midst of all this Mrs. Storrow decided that she needed a tiny chalet for her own use when she came to Switzerland—and it must be all ready for the opening, so that she could stay there!

Falk had been wondering if the big chalet was going to be ready—and now a new one was to be built!

The architect was summoned, the site was chosen, the workmen started to build and—when the Great Day came—there was the Baby Chalet all complete with two bedrooms, two bathrooms and sitting room.

Falk got up very early that morning in July and

looked out of the window. After all the rain the sky was blue and clear, and she murmured "God has given us a new day—for the sake of our house."

What a wonderful day it was, too!

Swiss Guides in their bright blue blouses covered the hillside "like Gentians"; the villagers came in their hundreds; as well as many famous people in the Guide world, including of course the Founder and the World Chief Guide—and the Fairy Godmother herself.

Our Chalet has been for the Guides and Girl Scouts of the world, all and more than its donor ever visualized.

Every year thousands of them come to work and play together there; to walk in the mountains and to make friends.

You can climb and ski, as Falk had hoped; and I think, too, you can find peace for the soul among the high alps.

High Days and Holidays

Building Headquarters

It has been related how, in 1910, Miss Baden-Powell rented a room from the Boy Scouts to serve as Girl Guide Headquarters. At the same time she engaged a secretary, Miss Macdonald, at a salary of £91 a year.

The money which started off the Association was provided by a loan of £100 from the Chief Scout, and so well did Miss Macdonald manage this small sum that by 1912 the loan was repaid. Indeed, the financial situation was so satisfactory that the Headquarters committee felt justified in expending as much as £1.7.6 in having the office re-painted, and an extra 10/- for whitewashing the ceiling. They also rose to the dignity of a brass plate, at a cost of 12/6, which was placed beneath that of the Boy Scouts at the entrance to the building.

The room was divided down the middle with a hessian screen; on one side was "the office" where Miss Macdonald sat at her desk, and on the other was "the shop" where the equipment was kept. When the Headquarters Committee held a meeting, Miss Macdonald was obliged to retire to the passage to interview callers.

In 1916 a disaster occurred; Headquarters was burnt out as a result of a fuse in the wiring of one of the

Scouts' rooms, and the Guides were forced to look for a new home. They moved to what must then have appeared to them very spacious premises—a flat at 76 Victoria Street. The kitchen served as a packing room, the drawers of the dresser being just the place for badges and emblems, while more stock was kept in the pantry. The files were stored in the bath!

This seemed a good idea at the time, but unfortunately the taps started to drip, and by the time this was discovered piles of correspondence had been reduced to a swampy pulp and many interesting records of the early days were lost forever.

Spacious as the flat at first appeared it was not long before it, too, became rather cramped with the work of the rapidly expanding movement, and in June 1920, the Guides were on the move again, to 25 Buckingham Palace Road this time, where the Scouts rented them a whole floor, they did not then require, in their fine new building. But they also were growing apace, and by 1929 the house which originally seemed big enough for both Associations was found to be barely sufficient for one.

What should be done?

The Executive Committee looked around for suitable offices, but could find nothing under £6,000 a year—a far cry from their first home at 15/- a week. So they took a deep breath and said, "Let's build our own Headquarters."

It was a bold decision, for the cost was estimated at £75,000; but in the long run it would be cheaper than renting, for the building would belong to them.

Moreover, they felt sure that the Guides and Brownies and Rangers would help . . . and so they did,

not only those living in Great Britain, but those
throughout the Commonwealth and even in other
countries.

A "brick" for Headquarters cost 2/6, and soon
Companies and Packs were busily engaged in paying for
as many bricks as possible for their new house. One
Brownie hearing about the scheme thought deeply, and
turned up at the next meeting with a real brick, which
was sent along for luck.

19, Buckingham Palace Road

For £2.10.0 a step of a staircase could be built; from
£5 to £50 supplied a window or door; counties pooled
their resources and gave whole rooms; the Chief Scout
and the Chief Guide gave the entrance doors . . . and so
it went on.

By March, 1931, the building was finished and the Queen herself came to open it. She was received by her daughter, Princess Mary, President of the Girl Guides, who handed her a golden key with which she opened the front door.

After a ceremony in the entrance hall, in which the Bishop of London pronounced the Blessing, Queen Mary made a tour of inspection. First she visited the kitchen on the top floor, where she looked in cupboards and examined the crockery—she banged a cup down on a table to make sure that it was good and strong!—then she proceeded to every single room in the whole of that huge building, asking questions and looking at every piece of furniture.

There was one incident which will never be forgotten.

Princess Mary had visited the old Headquarters on a previous occasion when, to the acute embarrassment of the Editor of *The Guide*, a cupboard filled to over-flowing with files and manuscripts had suddenly given way and, the doors springing open, had deposited the contents at Her Royal Highness's feet.

Now at the opening of the New Headquarters the Queen, with a knowing smile, asked to see inside the famous cupboard . . . it was opened . . . and was still filled to bursting point! The next day a new cupboard was delivered with Queen Mary's compliments.

The Ring of Adventurers

It has never been explained why the Girl Guides celebrated their twenty-first birthday in 1932, because the Association was officially founded in 1910, and the first Girl Scouts were already active in 1908. Whatever the reason for the choice of date the occasion was one of great rejoicing. Beacons were lit on hill-tops, avenues of cherry trees were planted, and parties of all kinds were attended with fun and merriment.

The serious side of Guiding was not forgotten and religious services, great and small, were held throughout the length and breadth of the land.

In "Guide Week", 22nd–29th May, companies and packs as well as individual Rangers, Guides and Brownies, set out to do extra special good turns to their families, their friends and their communities; it was a time, as the Chief Guide wrote later, of glorious generosity.

An event such as a Coming-of-Age is an occasion for looking back at the past, and this was no exception. The pioneers of the movement were now middle-aged ladies and, as is often the way with middle-aged ladies, some of them were inclined to sigh for "the good old days" and to say that the adventure had gone out of the game; everything was now so well organized that Guiding had become tame and dull.

Where were they, those glorious days when one went out into the blue to camp without the faintest idea of how to pitch a tent? Nowadays, they complained, a battery of Camp Advisers would prevent one taking the smallest risk of that kind, and so many pits were required for the disposal of refuse, greasy water and so on that a camp site was no better than a series of man-traps.

Not all the old-stagers felt like this, and one in particular, the Editor of *The Guide*, was quite certain that the spirit of adventure was still very much alive, and she set out to prove it.

She had a red car called Gulliver, and she announced

in *The Guide* one week that Gulliver would be
travelling in a certain neighbourhood and any Guides
who liked could come along and join in an impromptu
camp fire.

Nervously she wondered if anybody would accept the
invitation, but she need not have worried. The Guides
turned up in their hundreds. So Gulliver became a
regular rallying point; there was just a notice in *The
Guide*, giving time and place, and along they came, on
foot or cycle, in cars and buses. There was no
organization for getting them there, no coaches laid on
or Guiders chivvying them to a central meeting place.
They just came on their own initiative—and what
wonderful camp-fires those were! "We are the Ring of
Adventurers" they sang, for that is what they called
themselves, and that is what they were.

The Ring of Adventurers led on to the "Christmas
Stocking Trail". Again the Editor would announce the
route a car would take to collect Christmas Stockings
for children in hospital, or children who were suffering
through the curse of unemployment, which was
widespread at that time.

Guides, Brownies and Rangers looked eagerly in *The
Guide* each week to see if the route came anywhere
near their homes and then they would set out with their
gifts and wait patiently by the roadside.

The Christmas Stocking Trail was much too much for
Gulliver to take on alone, and hundreds of cars were
pressed into service to deal with the flood of presents.

It was such fun that nobody could bear to wait a year
until the following Christmas to do it all over again, so
several more "Trails" were "laid" in the intervening
months, to collect such things as eggs for old people or

comforts for hospital patients. Indeed these Trails only
came to an end with the outbreak of war.

The Cruise of the Calgaric

Another adventure of quite a different kind was
planned for the grown-ups. As usual, it was the Chief
Guide's idea but we should now call her The World
Chief Guide.

During one of the sessions of the Sixth World
Conference at Foxlease she was called away to the
telephone, and when she came back she was told, "We
want you to be our World Chief Guide!" She felt this to
be a tremendous honour, but also a tremendous
responsibility. No particular duties were laid down—just
to help Guiding all over the world all the time! And she
has done just that ever since, for she rarely rests from
her travels. Wherever she goes she leaves renewed
enthusiasm among the Guides and Girl Scouts who
often travel hundreds of miles to meet her at big rallies
or at little wayside stations where it is known that her
train will stop for a few minutes.

Speaking one day of her travels and how lucky she
and the Founder were to be able to meet so many
members of "their family" in their own countries, she
said, "If only I could take you all with me!" And then
the idea came. To get a ship and pack it full of Scouters
and Guiders and go for a cruise!

So it was that on August 12th, 1933, the White Star
liner *Calgaric* sailed down Southampton Water on her
way to the Baltic Sea.

The first port of call was Rotterdam. Scouts and
Guides packed on the quay side, eager to catch a
glimpse of their Chiefs—Lord and Lady Baden-Powell—

and as soon as they saw them on the boat deck they gave them a terrific reception, cheering, yelling and singing. Dutch Leaders then came on board to take their guests ashore for a wonderful day of sight-seeing and parties, before they sailed away, through the Kiel Canal, to Gdynia. Here the port was alive with Polish boys and girls, many of whom had travelled eight hours from distant parts of the country to be present on this historic occasion.

The cruisers were entertained to luncheon in a nearby Girl Scout camp; the Chiefs sat at a wonderful round table, cut out of the sand, which was decorated with beautiful and intricate patterns made up of pine-cones, beech-masts, pebbles and other natural objects. Before each tent the crest of the Province from which the Scouts came was drawn out in the same way; Warsaw for instance had a castle and Pomerania a mermaid.

This form of decoration is a speciality of the Baltic countries, and arriving in Lithuania the visitors were amazed to find all the paths through the woods, where this camp was sited, bordered by exquisite designs in which the initials B.-P. and the world trefoil were the principal motifs.

A public holiday had been decreed by the Government in honour of the cruise, and B.-P. performed the opening ceremony of a new street named after himself in a sea-side resort nearby. After this the President handed Lady Baden-Powell into a high-riding carriage, while B.-P., with the President's lady, entered another, then away they went across the sands at a hand gallop, the horses being driven on a loose rein in the Russian manner.

It was in this spectacular manner that the Chiefs and

their host and hostess arrived at the rally of 2,000 boys and girls which took place on the very edge of the tideless Baltic Sea.

The finale of the visit to Riga will never be forgotten by anyone who was there—the flaming sunset and the boats drifting down the river and out to sea to rejoin the *Calgaric,* accompanied by the strangely haunting melodies of Latvian folksongs sung by Scouts and Guides.

In Estonia the climax of the day was a gigantic campfire at which the Guides in their exquisitely embroidered national dresses danced and sang in the light of the flickering flames.

It was as well that nobody could look into the future, for within a few years Poland, Latvia, Lithuania and Estonia were to lose once more their recently attained freedom; their splendid Scouts and Guides were to be disbanded, and many of those who in 1933 pressed so eagerly around their Chiefs, laughing and cheering, were doomed to spend the rest of their lives in exile.

After a wonderful day in Helsinki the Chiefs were enthroned in a "bridal carriage" decorated with blue cornflowers and white asters—the Finnish colours. The cream-coloured pony was unharnessed and enthusiastic Scouts took his place between the shafts, and so the equipage arrived at the quayside. Here the Chiefs dismounted and proceeded on foot, shaking hands with everybody to right and left as they made their way on board.

This had an unforeseen result, as many of the lucky Scouts refused to wash the hand that "he" had shaken! It was only when desperate parents promised to bottle the water and keep it as a souvenir that the boys consented to submit to a scrubbing.

The Chief Guide of the National Association of

Sweden welcomed the visitors to Stockholm with an amusing speech in which she said, "Many centuries ago we people of the North visited you in a whole fleet of Viking ships, now you are returning the visit, but you bring friendship instead of bows and arrows, good will instead of burning boats; you take away a strong feeling of understanding instead of stolen treasure. How much nicer you are than we were!"

The day ended with the Scouts, in their exuberance, tossing B.-P. in a blanket before the anxious eyes of his wife. The girls were more restrained and contented themselves with carrying the Chief Guide shoulder high, in which exalted position she seemed quite at home.

The mountains of Norway were a new delight to the party, for all the other places they had seen had been flat plains and beaches. Here they sat under a starlit sky and looked down on the twinkling lights of Oslo far beneath, while above them on the hillside were thousands of bare-headed, flaxen-haired young Norwegians, their eyes fixed on the Chief Scout.

A few days later the *Calgaric* docked at Liverpool, and there drawn up to meet her was a body of smartly uniformed Scouts with a row of Guiders faultlessly attired in the background.

The passengers leant over the side of the ship shouting and waving, but the Guard of Honour, standing strictly to attention, looking at them in rather a strange way—at least so the puzzled cruisers thought. Then they realized what had happened—it was not their compatriots who had changed, it was they themselves, for in the course of their holiday they had shed every vestige of British reserve and had become quite continental in their habits!

Liverpool did them proud, the Lord Mayor coming on board to welcome them home, but when the train pulled in at Euston Station they looked in vain for the reception committee to which they had grown accustomed at every stopping place. London pursued the even tenor of its way quite unimpressed by the notables descending on No. 1 platform.

This would never do!

Mrs. Mark Kerr and her assistant County Commissioner leapt from the train, ran quickly to the barrier and returned as pompously as possible. "We have great pleasure," they announced to the Chiefs, "in welcoming you and your friends to London, and we hope you will enjoy your stay in our great city."

It was thus that this marvellous cruise came to an end—but already the participants were planning the next one, which in fact took place the following summer, when the Mediterranean countries received the cruisers with equal enthusiasm.

Coronation Celebrations

"Halt, who goes there?"

"A King's Messenger with greetings to His Majesty King George VI."

"Who carries on this message?"

"I do."

"Speed on, King's Messenger. God Save the King."

This ceremony was repeated hundreds of times as one messenger passed on to another the New Zealand Guides' loyal greeting to their new King. The message itself, based on the traditional Maori greeting to a Chief, began thus:

"To our illustrious Chief beyond the seas, the Centre

Pole of the Empire...We greet you and your Greenstone Ornament, our Gracious Queen and your children. This is but the small voice of your children of Ac-tea-wa, an outpost of your Empire, giving expression to their joy and gladness on your Coronation Day."

With the message went a sheepskin tanned down to fine vellum, on which was painted a map of New Zealand and pictures of Guides using every form of transport from their own legs to aeroplanes.

There was also a parchment signed by the Mayor of each place, who affixed the seal of his borough or city.

The map, message and parchment were carried in a three-foot long copper cylinder which was encased in a canvas envelope with a shoulder strap bearing a label inscribed "King's Messenger—Free Transport". This gave the messenger the right to travel free by courtesy of the Government, on all railway and service cars. Furthermore, the Minister of Education granted leave from school for each messenger whilst engaged on "The King's Business".

Sometimes the cylinder was handed over at a great gathering in some large city; sometimes before a small group of Guides and Brownies at a lonely station away in the country where even the impatient expresses had to wait until the ceremony was completed. In one place the greeting was carried on the back of a swimmer, in another it travelled in a Maori Princess's war canoe; at other times it was carried on horseback, by bicycle, or on foot. After covering 3,000 miles in New Zealand the message took ship for Great Britain where it was finally received by Their Majesties King George VI and Queen Elizabeth.

Guides in other parts of the Commonwealth

celebrated the Coronation in different ways. London staged a monster Rally at Wembley Stadium, where 13,000 Guides gave displays, while 80,000 from all over the country came to watch. A Commonwealth camp was held at the new camping site, Chigwell Row in Essex; while in Sydney, Australia, 3,000 Guides took part in a Rally at the end of which the whole 3,000 formed a World Trefoil in the centre of the arena—a most effective finale.

Scotland had a highly successful camp that summer of 1937, which synchronized with the meeting of the World Committee in Blair Castle. The foreign guests had a particular thrill when Lady Baden-Powell was piped on to the ground for the Perthshire County Rally by four Scottish Pipers in full dress.

Switzerland invited twenty-eight Guiders from fourteen countries to their national camp, and the Norwegian "open" Association included contingents from nine countries in their camp for 1,500.

The British Guiders and Rangers were very much impressed by the degree of responsibility taken by the Norwegian Patrol Leaders, and also by the ease and efficiency with which the huge camp was struck. Each Guide packed all her belongings, including bedding, in her rucksack, and strapping the tent on top shouldered the whole load and marched away. Thus practically the whole of the equipment was removed from the site in a few minutes.

Another splendid affair of 1937 was the United States Silver Jubilee Camp at Camp Andrée, near New York. Seventy-six Americans from all the States entertained twenty-six guests from twenty-six countries, all expenses being borne by the Juliette Low World

Friendship Fund. How Mrs. Low would have rejoiced to
see them there!

The selection of languages and the attempt to talk
them was truly reminiscent of the special Chalet
language, christened by Falk 'desperanto'.

One American Scout who "was fortunate," she said,
"in sitting next to the only girl who spoke no English
at all," tried describing a mosquito net in French and
terrified her neighbour by conveying the impression that
this flimsy piece of material was designed "to keep out
an animal likely to eat you."

After three glorious weeks of learning one another's
songs and dances and sampling one another's national
dishes, the whole party moved on to Pine Tree Camp in
Massachusetts, Aunt Helen Storrow's special preserve.

The all-day journey was far from dull, for the
"motorcade" was headed by police escorts, and Girl
Scouts greeted them at every stopping place.

The highlight of this week was a "New England
Clambake" (including lobsters) on the seashore.

One evening Aunt Helen with a partner gave a
demonstration of ballroom dancing. "She danced the
foxtrot, waltz and tango, with all the modern steps,
gracefully and with ease," wrote a Swedish Guide.
"Later we ourselves had a lesson and then we realized
how intricate the steps were."

Mrs. Storrow at this time was seventy-five years old,
and happily had several more dancing years ahead of
her.

Stormclouds

The Old Chief Goes Home

The highwater mark of Guiding seemed to have been reached in 1937. So far there had been no real set-back, but in 1938 Dame Katharine reported to the Tenth World Conference at Adelboden that the World Association had suffered severe losses amongst its Tenderfoot Member Countries.

This was a particular grief for Mrs.˙Kerr who since 1932 had been Commissioner for Tenderfoot Member Countries (now called "Associated Member Countries") and had loved and cherished her "babies"—who were not yet quite strong enough to become full members—like a real mother. It was, however, no fault of hers, nor of the Guides themselves, that caused this sad falling away.

Portugal had closed down her companies and packs in face of a newly established national youth movement; Austria had been incorporated ruthlessly into the German Reich, with the consequent disembodiment of her Association; in war-torn China the little body of Guides had dwindled to a mere handful.

"The influence of the national youth movements of Germany and Italy," Dame Katharine reported, "has inspired other governments to follow their example . . . It is now a reproach to be international."

Even in Great Britain the idea was mooted of a national youth movement to take the place of the numerous voluntary associations such as the Scouts and Guides, but luckily nothing came of it.

The last and greatest of the international camps before the lights went out in Europe, was the "Pax Ting", or Peace Parliament, which took place at Gödöllö near Budapest, from July 25th to August 7th 1939. In spite of the threat of war—which was in fact to break out only a month later—the Hungarians with great faith and courage carried on with their plans and 4,000 Guides and Girl Scouts from thirty-two countries came together for a perfect fortnight of sunshine and happiness, fun and friendship.

In the dark days of the following winter some of the French *Eclaireuses* who had attended the Pax Ting said to their Leader, "How happy we are to have this memory!" and the Leader added, "and this hope—for what has once been will surely be again."

The only thing that marred the Pax Ting itself was the absence of the Chiefs. It was the first time they had missed an important world event, but the Chief Scout had been in bad health for some time past, and now his doctors had ordered him a complete rest.

In the summer of 1938 he had taken part in the third British Scouters' and Guiders' Cruise, which visited Iceland, Norway, Denmark and Belgium, but he had not been well enough to go ashore. He appeared, however, on deck at each port, and so his Scouts and Guides in those countries saw him for the last time smiling happily as he acknowledged their greetings.

It was a time of world crisis when a Union Castle liner steamed slowly down Southampton Water on a dark foggy evening in the autumn of 1938 carrying B.-P. on his last voyage. He was leaving forever his home in England, Pax Hill, for his home in Kenya, Paxtu, which he had built for himself and his wife in the continent that he loved so dearly and which held for him so many memories.

As the two Chiefs watched the shores of England fade into the night they thought sadly of their great family of boys and girls, scattered over so many lands, soon to be engulfed in the most terrible war the world had ever known.

He was eighty-one, old in years though young in spirit, and he would not live to see what the end of it would be, nevertheless he had faith that Scouting and Guiding would survive and would help to build a better world when the fighting was over.

He died on January 8th 1941. The Scouts of Nyeri drew him to his last resting place. Over his grave stands a stone engraved with the Scout arrow-head and the Guide trefoil, and the words "Robert Baden-Powell, Chief Scout of the World".

War

The declaration of war in September, 1939, shook the movement to its foundations.

In Great Britain, London and other large cities were left, almost overnight, without a single company or pack, while country companies swelled to enormous proportions with the influx of evacuees brought out to areas considered safer from air-raids. Many Guiders left home to take up war work, but most of the companies carried on valiantly under Patrol Leaders. By degrees the turmoil of the early months subsided and "Guiding as

usual" became the order of the day, but with far more
emphasis on service. Guides took on every kind of job
that came to hand, from rolling bandages to bringing in
the harvest, from sorting salvage to amusing children in
play centres. It was all very much like 1914 but on a
vastly bigger scale.

Guides helping evacuees from Manchester

There were many stories of the heroism of Guides in
the face of danger; typical of them all, perhaps, was that
of the fourteen-year-old who joined a group of people

watching a large building which had been set alight by fire-bombs. The grown-ups hesitated to plunge into the smoke until they heard a voice cry out, "I am a Guide and I *will* not be afraid"; then a small figure rushed into the burning house; the others followed, the flames were extinguished and the building saved.

This Guide spoke for others all over the world who faced even greater dangers and suffering than the girls of Great Britain. Through letters which came by devious routes, and through the stories of people who escaped to comparative safety, it was learnt how the Promise and Law and the Guide training had enabled many a girl to endure bravely the terrifying ordeals which warfare must always bring to millions of unhappy people.

"Our country is in vital need of an Air Ambulance Service," wrote the Chief Commissioner in *The Guider* for April 1940. She went on to add that two machines then in the course of construction would cost £15,000, and mentioned an additional £5,000 to pay for a life-boat.

"In the last war," she continued, "we raised £2,500 . . . there were only 50,000 of us then. Now there are over half a million in Great Britain alone! . . . and we want to raise £20,000. Can we do it? Of course we can!"

Of course they could! By the end of Guide Gift Week more than twice that sum had been subscribed from all over the Commonwealth, and so in addition to the air ambulances and the life-boat, twenty motor ambulances were presented to the Navy; two mobile canteens were given to the Army; and the Trefoil Hut in Iceland was furnished and equipped for the Merchant Navy.

This was only the beginning of the money earned and

saved by Guides, Brownies and Rangers for the use of people whose need was greater than their own.

A fund of £100,000 was built up in memory of the Founder, which was invested at the time and is now used to help the cause of international friendship, by enabling Guides and their Leaders to go abroad to camps and conferences, and by helping visitors from other countries to come to Great Britain.

The best stunt connected with the raising of this fund took place on February 20th, 1942, when the Army Pigeon Service provided "homers" to carry Thinking Day Greetings from all the various counties to the Chief Guide in London, for Lady Baden-Powell had returned from Kenya to receive the warmest of warm welcomes from her Guides in Great Britain.

A bunch of excited people stood on the roof of Pigeon Headquarters eagerly gazing at the sky for the first speck to come nearer and nearer, and finally become recognizable as a "homer". When you look hard at the sky you start seeing spots whether there is anything there or not! So it was on this occasion, but at last—yes—it really was a pigeon coming in to land!

Seeing the unexpected crowd, however, the bird thought better of it, and circled round suspiciously, again and again.

After an agonizing ten minutes the army pigeoneers told everyone else to hide among the chimney-pots while they rattled tins of corn and called out in soothing pigeon-language. The homer alighted on a roof-top, but was still rather suspicious, playing "bo-peep" coyly around the chimney cowls. Finally he decided that all was well and hoppity-hop he went through the little trap-door. Then the message was taken from his leg and handed to Lady Baden-Powell:

"These messengers flying from your birthplace—Chesterfield—take Derbyshire's thoughts and prayers to all Guides to form a strong link in the chain of Guiding round the world."

The Queen, then Princess Elizabeth, and Princess Margaret preparing their Thinking Day Greetings for the Chief Guide

Later on there arrived the pigeon sent off from Yorkshire by the Princess Royal, and then those released by Princess Elizabeth and Princess Margaret.

The two Princesses had been enrolled, the one as a Guide and the other as a Brownie, in the 1st Buckingham Palace Company and Pack in 1937, and had been as keen as possible on Guiding ever since. When, at the outbreak of war, the members of this company dispersed, the Princesses started a new one at Windsor among the children of the employees on the estate.

They were a real out-of-door group, hiking and camping in the grounds and taking particular pleasure in swinging themselves over a "commando" course that they had constructed, which was a pretty strenuous athletic feat.

They were also keen on stalking. There was one incident which caused great amusement. The King himself came unexpectedly one day to see how the Guides were getting along, and surprised the Captain lying full length among the bracken, apparently asleep (so he contended) although *she* insisted she was just acting as a stalking target! Anyway, she was very much chaffed for long afterwards on the way she conducted a Guide meeting!

Later on the Princesses became Sea Rangers, and were among the first, with the rest of their crew, to take a course on board the M.T.B. training ship moored in the River Dart, which had been acquired by the Girl Guides in 1946.

It was no wonder that the Princesses were keen Guides for their mother, Queen Elizabeth, had been a Commissioner before her marriage. To-day she is Patron of the Girl Guides Association, together with her daughter the Queen, while Princess Margaret is President, having accepted this appointment on the death of the Princess Royal in 1965.

Among all the societies which they support and encourage with their Patronage the Guides still retain a place of great affection in their hearts.

The G.I.S.

"We must look to the future and prepare ourselves for the time to come," wrote Mrs. Mark Kerr in *The Guider* of February 1941. "More important even than winning the war is the question of winning the peace. In fact there will be no use in winning the war unless we can do better with the ensuing peace that we did last time."

She went on to suggest that volunteers should at once start to train for service in the countries over-run by the fighting, so that they might be ready to bring what help and comfort they could to the suffering people as soon as hostilities ceased. Several others wrote letters supporting the scheme and giving further suggestions.

The idea was received with the greatest enthusiasm by all members of the movement from the youngest Brownie upwards; thousands of Guiders offered their services and the only difficulty was the matter of selection.

A committee was formed to make practical plans, to contact the Government authorities and to get advice from societies with experience of relief work.

It was thus that the G.I.S. was born. The Guide International Service (British) was the official title, usually shortened to G.I.S.(B) which provided the original name of "Gisby" for a certain small baby in a refugee camp in Germany, whose admiring godmothers were of course team members.

The Society of Friends, from its long experience,

advised, "take only those prepared to do the impossible," and added that the motive for volunteering was all important. Those who were attracted only by the honour and glory or the adventure of the undertaking were not accepted for the glory would wear thin in surroundings of dirt and illness, and the adventure would peter out in monotonous routine work. The only acceptable motive was the real desire to serve without expecting any thanks or any reward.

A very large sum was needed to equip the teams with all they needed in the way of medical and hospital supplies, clothing and food, as well as the motor caravans to transport them. There was no difficulty in raising it, for the Guides and Brownies of the Commonwealth rose, as they always do, to the occasion and within two years subscribed £112,000 and sent, in addition, many useful gifts in kind.

The training for the team members was as arduous as it could be. In order to toughen themselves physically they camped in the Welsh mountains in mid-winter and dragged loaded trek-carts for miles over the roughest ground they could find. If anyone were going to break under the strain, they thought, it was better to do so before she got on to the real job, where a replacement would mean delay and the consequent neglect of vital work.

Besides learning, or improving, technical skills, so that they could cook, nurse, doctor, organize and so on in the most difficult circumstances imaginable, they also studied the history, culture, traditions and language of the countries they were likely to visit. However clever you may be at your work you cannot do much for people unless they trust you, and you cannot really understand their needs unless you know something of their background.

The first team left England in June, 1944, for Egypt *en route* for Greece. They had many adventures, many difficulties to overcome, many problems to solve. They found that their training had not been in any way too rigorous, for the Greek mountains, where they worked for much of the time, were even wilder than Wales. The roads were appalling and the country in a state of chaos, as was only to be expected after years of war and enemy occupation; and within a few months of liberation the so-called civil war broke out.

One volunteer working in a little town away up in the mountains wrote home: "We have been snowed up for nearly a week ... we've finished our bread but have enough corned beef and biscuits ... We are trying to get workers to clear the road so that food convoys can get through ... our great problem is refugees who keep pouring into the town."

Some of them had been walking for weeks, often without shoes, over the snow-covered mountains, eating anything they could find, even grass. One lad, when he was given a piece of bread, kissed it and put it in his pocket, taking it out from time to time just to look at it. Bread has a special significance for Greeks, since it is taken at the Communion Service, and even a common loaf is looked upon, in a way, as holy.

One of the principal jobs was distributing clothing, and often the villagers though they had not enough to eat themselves, would try and express their gratitude by inviting the teams to share their meal, or would give them little presents of a few eggs or perhaps a live hen. The volunteers were very touched by these gifts, and although they hated to accept them they knew that to refuse would hurt the donors' feelings, so they just tried to take as little as possible.

The G.I.S. in Egypt, 1945

There were of course amusing incidents to lighten the day's work. There was the occasion when a group of homeless children was being flown to a place where they could receive greater care and attention than in the temporary camp where the G.I.S. team were looking after them. Before they could leave it was necessary to fill in the name of each one's nearest relative on an official form. These children had become separated from their families and nobody knew where to find them, even if they were still alive, so the team leader wrote her own name in every space reserved for "next-of-kin", amid much chaff from her colleagues on the sudden increase in her family.

Two teams followed immediately in the wake of the liberating armies who entered Holland the day before the armistice was declared. They received a tremendous welcome from the brave Dutch people whom they had come to help, but in some ways it was heart-breaking work. They had their orders, designed to fit in with those of other relief organizations.

Food and supplies were to be given to this particular village, but not to that one, which would be served by some other group. It was desperately hard, when they saw the urgent need, to refuse supplies to the first people they met, but they knew that if they disobeyed orders the confusion would be appalling. They had to remind themselves that the village they were bound for was in as great a state of distress, and pray that those they were obliged to refuse would understand and would be quickly served by their own appointed helpers.

A third team soon joined these first two, and later they all moved on into Germany. This contingent consisted of a mobile hospital and laboratory; a general relief team; and a kitchen and canteen team.

The state of the country was chaotic, for the tide of battle had swept over it leaving devastation in its wake. Many refugees were on the move trying to get back to their own countries; others had found their homes destroyed, and conditions even worse than in Germany, and so were returning to the Displaced Person's Camps, which were already overcrowded. All were in a wretched state, half-starved, ill and barely clothed.

The condition of the children was the most pitiable, and one G.I.S. volunteer remarked after months of attending to them, "I have forgotten what a well child looks like." They were pathetically grateful for the simplest toys, a rag doll maybe, made by a team member in an odd moment from an old ammunition bag—or for any clothes. One little Polish girl was seen to dance round and round in her new shoes, unable to believe in her luck.

Apart from illness, dirt was the worst problem, and so when a team arrived in any place its first job was usually to cart away rubbish and burn it, then to scrub and clean out a building of some sort before spraying everything within sight—including people—with D.D.T.

The work was far from glamorous or romantic, but it had to be done, and the volunteers needed all their determination to compete with the hardship and the suffering that they saw all around them. It was indeed a test of their Guide training in every way, and not one of them failed. They came from many different parts of the Commonwealth and all earned the affection and respect of the people among whom they worked, as well as high praise from the Authorities; but they never forgot that it was the Guides at home who kept them in the field.

The G.I.S. stayed in Germany until 1952 working amongst the refugees, helping them in every possible way, including the starting of Guides and Brownies in several camps. The lucky ones emigrated by degrees to other countries—Australia and New Zealand, North and

South America, Great Britain, Switzerland, and so on—to start their lives anew, but for some there was no chance of leaving owing to the fact that they were ill, or too old, or had too many small children. In these cases no country was willing to accept them, and they remained for years still living, some of them, in refugee camps, although the more fortunate ones were gradually re-housed in better conditions.

The G.I.S. teams were the very last of the relief workers to leave Germany, and they only left then because the Authorities ordered all such work to come to an end. In future, it was decreed, the German Government would be responsible for these unhappy exiles.

Australia and New Zealand each sent a team to work in Malaya, where, besides feeding and caring for the refugees, they had the fun of starting and running several Brownie Packs.

Conditions here were even worse, if possible, than in Europe.

The dreadful disease called Yaws is the curse of this part of the world, and the teams battled to cure it in thousands of men, women and children. It could be cured with arsenic injections (penicillin, which is also effective, had not yet been discovered), but there was an acute shortage of this essential medical supply. The teams had orders to treat only the selected few—children who were likely to recover. It was heart-rending for them to see patients whom they had to refuse to treat coming day after day to the clinic. Almost, the Guiders felt, it would be better if these long-suffering souls would complain or abuse them, but they never did; they just sat quietly and patiently waited, in case . . .

One man stood by the side of the road every Monday when their lorry passed on its way to the clinic. "If we get the medicine from Australia," they said, "we will treat you," and they went on, hoping and praying that it would arrive, for they could hardly bear to see him there each successive week. They had telegraphed to the Guides of Australia, a desperate message asking for more arsenic injections. Other people in Malaya thought the G.I.S. were mad even to hope. It was well known that all the stuff had been bought up and even if you could find any the price was fantastic. Imagine, then, how the team felt when, only a few days before they had orders to leave, the injections arrived! Somehow the Guides had done the trick when everyone else had failed . . . and this medicine was their own—not issued by the authorities—so they could use it as they liked. The patient waiters were rewarded, and on the following Monday the man by the roadside was given his injection. That was perhaps the happiest moment of all.

The Phoenix Rises from the Ashes

When the G.I.S. team arrived in Greece the last thing they expected to find was an active Guide Association, for they knew that the movement had been disbanded in 1939, so their astonishment was great when a young woman rushed up to them in Athens and shook them warmly by the left hand—the Scout and Guide handshake—and said that the Chief Commissioner had gone into the country on Guide business but would of course want to meet them as soon as she returned.

It was in 1930 that the seed of Guiding was sown in Greece, by some Greek Guides from Egypt who came to Athens for the Centenary of Greek Independence.

Little did these girls know, when they took part in a procession on a hot, dusty day that "their smiling faces and their proud, free bearing" would so impress the daughter of the Greek Chief Scout that she determined from that moment to start Guides in Greece.

Having followed them back to their hotel she talked to them, and later started up a correspondence with their Leader whom she persuaded to come over and settle in Athens in order to help with the training of Guiders.

Mrs. Kerr also had a finger in the pie, for she was a well-known Philhellene—or friend of Greece—and spoke Greek quite fluently. So Guiding got away to a flying start and Greece was soon accepted as a Tenderfoot member of the World Association.

Then the blow fell. The Government decided to ban all voluntary societies in favour of a big national youth movement.

A Guide of that time has described her company's last meeting as the sun set behind the purple mountains that ring Athens: "We hoisted our flag and renewed our Promise; and we said that although we could not meet again or wear our uniforms we would always be Guides in our hearts. Then we tried to sing our Guide song, only we could not sing very well because we were all crying too much."

So that was officially the end; but the spirit of Guiding lived on and when Greece was liberated it flared up and, like a bush fire, swept right across the land.

"I suppose every boy wants to help his country" are the opening words of *Scouting for Boys*, and these words were never more applicable than to the girls as well as the boys of Greece in 1944. There was so much to be done to rebuild their country, and they were all eager to help in every way they could.

Their Guide badge bears a Phoenix—the mythical bird which was burnt and rose again from the ashes—which is truly symbolical of the rebirth of Guiding after years of war and enemy occupation.

In 1939 there were approximately 3,000 Guides—in 1946 there were 10,000! And this in spite of the war that broke out within a few months of liberation, in which thousands of children were kidnapped and carried across the frontier behind the so-called "iron curtain", of whom only a few hundred ever returned to their own country.

In order to save their children from this fate many parents living in the northern villages sent them to the Children's Colonies which were started in the south and in the islands. The young women who volunteered to help in these colonies were trained by the Guide Association, who ran courses for them on the same lines as those for Guiders.

Some of the Greek Trainers had been to Foxlease, with the result that games familiar to English Guides are now played in the Greek mountains.

Scout troops and Guide companies, Wolf Cub and Brownie packs sprang up in the Colonies, and so the movement spread over the country when in 1949 the war ended and the children could go home.

Getting Together Again

Joys and Sorrows

St. George's Day, 1945, was the most wonderful day there has ever been for the French Scouts and Guides. Flags were unearthed from secret places and uniforms which had been hidden away for years were once more proudly worn by the boys and girls of Paris.

It did not seem possible for so many of them to appear correctly dressed at the great Rally on April 23rd, but there they were, swinging down the Champs-Elysees six abreast, saluting Lady Baden-Powell as they passed.

The Chief Guide had not waited for the end of the war to get across the Channel to visit her "family", and she was in fact in France when peace was declared. With her went Mrs. Leigh-White, who had succeeded Dame Katharine as Director of the World Bureau in 1938.

Rose Kerr had been eagerly looking forward to taking part in this tour, but she was not fated to see the coming of peace. She died in December, 1944; almost her last act was to send a telegram of rejoicing to her friends in Greece, whose country had just been liberated.

She was mourned by Guide Leaders around the world. Sweden expressed the feelings of all in a telegram which described her as a "Bridge between nations showing the way", and in the re-building of world Guiding in the following years her wise judgment was sorely missed.

Another great leader and pioneer died also about this time—Mrs. James Storrow. So the Guide Movement suffered a double loss just at the time when the clouds were lifting and the future seemed full of promise.

It must not be thought, however, that international Guiding came to an end during the war. Many Guides were among the refugees who escaped to Britain from Europe and British Guides did their best to make them welcome.

Golondrina is the Spanish word for "swallow", and at Mrs. Kerr's suggestion this was the name given to the Guides who came like the swallows for a brief visit before returning home once more. Nobody could foresee that many of them would never again see their own countries.

One *Golondrina* who was especially welcome was Olga Malkowska. She had brought the children of her school in Poland through danger to safety in a neutral country, and had then continued her journey to England. On arrival, she was decorated with the Bronze Cross, the British Guides' highest award for gallantry, which was presented to her by the Queen.

Mrs. Leigh-White had visited the Western Hemisphere in 1941, and had set up a branch office of the World Bureau in New York, which is still very active. The Girl Scouts of the United States increased enormously in numbers during the war years, and they sent many thousands of parcels to Guides in Great Britain to help them in the days of rationing and general shortages. Guides throughout the Commonwealth did likewise, and so the spirit of friendship grew with the years, and when peace came at last it seemed as if there were a surge forward as of a mighty river bursting through the dam that had held it back for so long, as Guides hurried to renew personal contacts.

The World Committee met in 1945; all the members were still alive, although some had suffered terribly, and this was a very touching meeting of old friends. In 1946 the World Conference was held at Evian in France and it may be imagined how eagerly news was exchanged and plans for the future made.

Great Britain invited several countries to send mixed teams of Scouts and Guides to take part in a folk-dancing festival, and it seemed quite like old times to see again the lovely national dresses of Czechoslovakia, Belgium, Holland, Denmark and France mingling with the saffron of the Ulster team, the green of the Americans, the tartans of the Scots and the tall hats of Wales. England always comes off badly in these affairs, having no traditional dress, but the Scout Morris dancers looked very gay with their ribbons and bells.

As Guides and their friends watched the dances, one lovely summer's day in Hyde Park, it seemed that nothing but happiness lay ahead.

More sorrow, however, was in store. Within a year Poland, Hungary and Czechoslovakia were to join the Baltic countries behind the Iron Curtain, and their Guides and Scouts were to be disbanded.

We shall never forget them and one day we feel sure we shall welcome them back into our World Association.

All Roads Lead to Oxford

What do you think of when somebody says "Oxford"? An ancient university? Lost causes? Motor cars? The Boat race?

In 1950 every Guide would have said "Scrolls".

After twenty years the World Conference was once again taking place in England—at the very same place as the first one, St. Hugh's College, Oxford, and the Guides of Great Britain were all agog.

This was an opportunity not to be missed, for what could be easier than to give every delegation to the conference a message of friendship to take back to the Guides of their own country?

So the Scrolls were prepared. Each one carried the same message, but the beautiful decorations were all different.

Perhaps it was the Guides of New Zealand and their Coronation Greeting who gave somebody the thought of sending these messages to Oxford by all possible forms of transport. They followed special routes traversing every county in the United Kingdom, and a log-book recorded the journey of each one as it passed through town and village and country, often spending the night in some historic building.

One message was flown most of the way, accompanied by Air Rangers; one came on horseback over the old pony tracks of the West Country; another crossed the Irish Channel from Ulster and continued along canals and waterways. Yet another came by bicycle, (even by an ancient "pennyfarthing" along one lap) while still another took a ride on the back of an elephant from the Edinburgh Zoo.

There can hardly have been a mayor or a policeman

in the country who had nothing whatever to do with this glorious affair as the Scrolls were handed on from Guide to Ranger, from Ranger to Brownie, on their way to Oxford.

An elephant from Edinburgh Zoo sets off with one of the scrolls

It was something of a triumph when every one arrived on the appointed day and, at an immense campfire attended by 10,000 Guides, was handed over to H.R.H. Princess Margaret who then presented it to the appropriate delegate to take back to her own country.

Several messages and log-books were received in

return by British Guides the following year, and an invitation to camp in Belgium was accepted with alacrity by the Welsh Guides.

Indeed one might say that the echoes of running feet have hardly yet died away.

The Director's Travels

In 1951 Dame Leslie Whateley was appointed Director of the World Bureau. She had not been a Guide, although her sister was a County Commissioner, and she herself said she hardly knew how she had escaped being involved in the Movement hitherto. She said too that the Promise. and Law expressed values she had always believed in, so she was enrolled in the presence of the British Executive Committee, and from that moment threw herself heart and soul into the work of the World Association.

Like Dame Katharine she had had a distinguished war-time career, having been the head of the Women's Auxiliary Territorial Service, and with the coming of peace she determined to devote herself to furthering international understanding.

During her thirteen years in the job she visited nearly every Member Country of the World Association, often more than once, not only making friends with the heads of the national organizations but also visiting Companies and Packs in the remote parts of the country.

She became quite used to unusual forms of transport. Once in South Africa her plane to a distant village was piloted by a seventeen-year-old Sea Scout with a fifteen-year-old Scout navigator, but this was a luxurious journey compared to most.

The question of transport presents an incredible

picture to those who live in countries where buses ply regularly from city to city and where a large proportion of the population possesses mechanically reliable cars to drive on first class roads.

Here is a brief description taken from *The Council Fire*, of an expedition to visit Guides in one of the African countries. It is typical of many such undertaken by Dame Leslie in different continents.

"The Director is touring Africa studying problems, giving practical advice, making friends with Guide people, helping to recruit Leaders. This is important for how can help be given unless the problems are known? There is much that cannot be told through correspondence, particularly where language barriers exist and where, in out-lying places, there is even a literacy problem.

So the Director is in Africa and with the local Commissioner plans to visit a number of villages where communications are almost non-existent. There is no post, no telephone, no telegraph. The only way of contacting the Guides is to go to them. The road is so dangerous that it is closed from dusk to dawn.

With some difficulty a car for hire is found. Do you visualise a shining Cadillac? Think again! The bonnet is tied on with string.

The interior – one cannot describe it as upholstery – is held in place by Sellotape. The radiator leaks and has to be filled every twenty minutes from a not-so-nearby river with a little old pint-size can. The windows disappeared long ago and a sudden storm half-drowns the occupants.

The Director and Commissioner set forth at dawn. As they pass through each village they call out 'Back later to see the Guides!'' And I reckon they have their fingers crossed in case their vehicle breaks down for good.

The return journey finds little groups of excited children awaiting them. Indeed the whole village turns out, for a visitor is a distinct rarity. Guiding is given a tremendous fillip public relations-wise. The village is impressed. Support will be forthcoming in the future.''

On this journey, as on many another, Dame Leslie was presented with gifts at each village—gifts such as a live hen or two, eggs (unwrapped of course), extra-ripe fruit—from the delighted inhabitants. You are left to imagine the state of her pale blue summer uniform on her return to town after bumping over dust-filled pot-holes – not forgetting that thunderstorm – with the eggs making an omelette in her lap, hens flapping and squawking and shedding feathers, and the fruit, having burst its banks, so to speak rolling around all over the place.

Dame Leslie did more than can be told for international Guiding with her great talent for making friends, through her wise advice and her never-failing sense of humour. She did much too for the Boy Scouts wherever she went, and they thought so highly of her that the Scout World Committee awarded her the Bronze Wolf "for outstanding service to the Movement". Only 39 people had been thus honoured previously, and only one of these had been a woman. You can easily guess who she was—Lady Baden-Powell of course!

Our Chalet Comes of Age
The year 1952 was packed with great occasions. First of all came the Coming-of-Age of Our Chalet.

Guide Leaders from all over the world converged on the little village of Adelboden, where every hotel had its quota of guests, for there were far too many for all to find beds in the Guide House.

In the valley behind Our Chalet the green grass was dotted with tents, those of Finland shaped like Eskimo igloos exciting much interest.

The flags of half a dozen countries proclaimed the presence of Guides and Rangers from various parts of Europe, while at the head of the valley, beneath the towering height of the Lohner and close beside the great Bonder waterfall, was the International Drama Camp. Here were 43 young Guiders from 26 countries spread over every continent, whose aim was to prepare an entertainment, themselves making all the costumes and props, for the Birthday Party. The fact that there was not one language which could be understood by everyone was of no consequence, "Desperanto" filling in all the gaps. The music for the entertainment was provided by the International Singing Camp, which was lodged in one of the hay chalets in the valley.

The day of the party was grey and cloudy, and as the thousands of guests assembled on the hillside some heavy drops of rain splashed down causing umbrellas to be hastily opened. Happily, however, the Clerk of the Weather suddenly changed his mind and everyone breathed a sigh of relief.

As is usual on these occasions there were many fine speeches from all sorts of important people, including the World Chief Guide. Then gifts were presented to the Chalet and also to Falk, who was celebrating her own birthday as well as the end of her service as Guider-in-Charge.

Luges decorated with wild flowers were dragged in by the "second generation" of Cubs and Brownies whose mothers were in camp; a simply wonderful cake, made in the form of Our Chalet, was given by the people of the village; and there were many more presents too numerous to describe. Suddenly there was a zooming sound and everyone looked up at the sky to see a small aeroplane circling above the crowd. As it passed over the Chalet for the third time it dropped a parcel almost at Falk's feet. This turned out to contain railway and steamer tickets with an invitation to visit the Scandinavian countries.

Then came tea and a buzz of conversation. Swiss Guides with big baskets strapped to their backs acted as mobile litter bins, attracting much custom, and when the last carton was discarded and the last cake eaten everyone sat down again to enjoy the entertainment.

Solemn gentlemen in top-hats argued around a conference table. All wanted to bring peace to the world, but not one was willing to make any sacrifice to attain it.

Then the scene shifted to a market-place. A gipsy was telling fortunes with a pack of cards, and the passers-by were invited to try their luck.

The Ace of Clubs was the lucky card, which, she foretold, would bring peace to the world, for what is the ace of clubs but the Guide trefoil?

Turning their eyes to the Chalet the audience now saw the shutters swing open to reveal in each window a Guide from a different country.

It was a lovely ending and everyone realized that here, at Our Chalet, it was indeed true that no national rivalries existed, because everyone belonged to the same

Guide family.

This friendly atmosphere, sensed by everyone who stays there, was originally created by Falk, and the tradition was carried on by her successor, Pen Wood-Hill, once International Secretary for Great Britain, who came to be known and loved by countless Guides and Guiders of all nationalities.

From Adelboden Lady B.-P. and some others flew on to Norway for the fourteenth world conference, and then hurried back to England for the big international camp organized by the British.

The village green—with of course its village shop—was the centre of the camp and here at all hours of the day Guides and Girl Scouts milled around and stood each other ice-cream in almost every language under the sun.

Thousands of Guides came to the big campfire and the Pageant called "The Golden Ball", the theme of which is the Golden Ball of Scouting which B.-P. tossed to the children of the world—a fitting climax to a memorable year.

The Coronation Tribute

The great event of 1953 for the whole of the Commonwealth was of course the Coronation of H.M. Queen Elizabeth.

The Guides showed their love and loyalty for the Queen, who had been one of them, in a specially Guide-like way. From Thinking Day, February 22nd, until Coronation Day, June 3rd, they set about helping other people in every way they could think of, either as individuals or in Patrols or even larger groups.

All over the Commonwealth Brownies, Guides, Rangers and Guiders set to work. They planted gardens

and painted railings to bring an air of gaiety to their
neighbourhood; they sent parcels to all sorts of lonely
people, including lighthouse keepers; they subscribed
money, in sums great and small, to many charities,
notably the Guide Dogs for the Blind and the Children's
Country Holiday Fund.

Outside Buckingham Palace with Coronation tributes in 1953

Brownies, as always, had the most original ideas. One
pack suggested cutting the toenails of all the old people
in the village who had grown too stiff to bend down.

Another Brownie, reversing the usual role, sat in with Grannie on Saturday night.

All who took part in this "Coronation Tribute of Service" wore a badge incorporating the Guide Trefoil and a Crown; and at the end of the period of service they wrote on special cards the list of good turns they had carried out in Patrols or Sixes. These cards were put in envelopes bearing a gaily coloured design of lambs, trees, and Guides and were sent through Districts and Counties to the Chief Commissioner who forwarded a few of them to the Queen. Nobody but the Chief Commissioner and the Queen know which were the cards to receive this distinction so every Guide Patrol and Brownie Six may think, "Perhaps it was ours!"

It was a Brownie who expressed every girl's feelings. She had done the household chores for an old lady—sweeping, washing up, making tea—and when she was thanked she replied, "But I didn't do it for you! I did it for the Queen!"

The World Today

Centenary Year

"It is your business in life to be happy . . . to bring happiness into the world by making happy homes."

These words taken from Baden-Powell's last message to the Guides inspired the World Committee's proposal that all members of the Movement might honour their Founder by commemorating the centenary of his birth in 1957 by doing extra good turns based on the theme "Homes of To-day and Tomorrow".

The World Bureau published a colourful leaflet explaining "Our home is our house—our community— our world" so it seemed that the sky was the limit.

Some countries organised a national project to meet a deeply-felt need either in their own land or for the under-privileged overseas; others threw out suggestions leaving it to the initiative of Brownies, Guides and Rangers to work out their own plans.

Only those who have travelled a hot, hypnotic dead straight road under the blazing sun can have any idea of the joy of seeing a group of wayside trees where the weary travellers can relax awhile in the welcome shade.

South Africans are among those who know what this means, and so the Guides put in hand a great tree-planting project.

Trees for shade, trees for beauty, trees to put a stop

to soil erosion, common trees and rare trees, forest trees and flowering trees, but mostly trees beginning with "B" and "P"—all these were planted throughout the length and breadth of the country, the Guides undertaking to care for them through the years ahead, often with the enthusiastic co-operation of the local authorities.

In the Cook Islands, far away in the Pacific Ocean, Guides set to work making patchwork quilts which they sent to New Zealand to be added to other parcels destined for Korea.

Pakistan Guides embarked on a grand literacy campaign "Each One Teach One". Three courses in adult literacy were begun in Karachi and Lahore, while individuals were taught to read and write and do simple accounts in their own homes. Experts from the Village Aid Institute and from UNESCO gave much help in this ambitious scheme and by the end of the year 1,000 adults had passed the literacy test and received their certificates.

Brownies, or Bluebirds as they are called in Pakistan, concentrated on the theme "Grow More Food" with the result that thousands of little gardens were dug and planted to supply fresh vegetables to the hungry.

Norway raised a large sum of money by means of a "Bob-a-Job Week" to buy flats for refugees in Austria; and the Netherlands gave a choice of three projects—a school for Arab children in Nazareth, a hospital in what was then called the Belgian Congo, or a plane for the use of missionaries in New Guinea.

In the United States the slogan "Keep America Beautiful" was interpreted by the Girl Scouts of Maryland in a drive to make litter-bags for every Scout family car.

In the United Kingdom, as in many other countries, it was left to local groups to decide on what needed to be done and it is difficult to know what to pick out for special mention.

A Post Ranger Group earned enough money to give a Polish girl a holiday from her refugee camp in Germany; a Guide group sought out and enlisted blood donors; two Brownies organized an animal service, feeding and exercising pets left behind when their owners went away for the holidays.

There were of course some slight mistakes resulting from over-enthusiasm. "Dad said it wasn't quite the colour he'd have chosen for the garden gate, but maybe it will tone down in time." "Granny said she couldn't settle if I kept shaking up her cushions." Still, it's the thought that counts!

"I fed the fouls when I could of been skatting on my roller skatts and I put my twin couseens to sleep." Let's hope that the "twin couseens" obliged and allowed the little African Brownie to return to her "skatting".

It is impossible to assess how many millions of good turns were accomplished nor to put a value on each. Who can say how digging a drain for a remote village compares with the effort "To get on better with my brothers and sisters"? Or whitewashing a church to the resolution "To do what I am told without arguing"?

What is encouraging is that many of the projects started in 1957 were carried on for many years—some even to the present day. As one Guide said "We couldn't stop visiting old Mrs. Smith and doing her shopping for her when she had come to depend on us."

Another idea for celebrating the Centenary was

inevitably a 'world camp. But the world being so vast and the expense of travel so great it was realised that only a limited number of Guides would be able to get together in the same place. What to do?

The problem was solved by a delegate from The Philippines attending the 1954 World Conference in Holland where the matter was being discussed.

"Why not have ONE World Camp" she said "in several PIECES?"

And so that is what happened.

Four countries each had a "piece" to organize. They were Canada, The Philippines, Switzerland and the United Kingdom.

Groups of Guides and Rangers from 25 countries travelled to The Philippines for the first camp which was held in tropical heat in January. Rockets soared into the sky to announce to the whole countryside the opening of this historic camp, and a representative from each of the foreign groups, armed with a golden bow, shot a golden arrow into the air.

For the British contingent camping in the tropics provided many new experiences. Water flowed to the five sub-camps through bamboo pipes and little bamboo bridges spanned the rivulets here and there; bamboo lamp-posts lit the paths at night, but best of all was the chance to sleep in a nippa hut instead of an oven-like canvas tent.

Who could possibly imagine a more beautiful spot for the Swiss Camp than the Vallée de Conches with the greyish, icy waters of the river Rhone always within sight and sound? And with the mountains silhouetted against the sky on either side?

The 'Gommer Express', the special Guide train,

dropped the campers off at intervals all down the valley, for the small sub-camps were strung out over six miles. Each group had its own programme of work-shops, dancing, singing and other activities, but the whole camp—5,000 Swiss and 1,000 visitors—came together for a huge camp-fire one evening where the greatest attraction was the World Chief Guide in person.

Nobody unless they have heard Lady Baden-Powell speak can have the slightest idea of how she always thrills an audience. She seems to be speaking to each person individually and her voice and expressive gestures tell the story even if the language is unfamiliar.

On this occasion she spoke in a mixture of French and English so that nearly everyone could understand her message which ended with the words "Happiness here in our camp will help you to spread this happiness in our homes . . . as we go forward with the idea of the spirit of the Movement *dans notre coeur*."

Cree, Bella Coola, Mic Mac, Iroquois—famous North American Indian tribes—provided names for the four sub-camps sited beside beautiful Doe Lake, 160 miles north of Toronto in thickly wooded, rolling country. Here 1,600 girls from 46 countries arrived by special train to live, work and play together for unforgettable days of fun and friendship.

The highlight for many of the visitors was Canada's traditional sport of canoeing. Those who passed the qualifying test—which included upsetting a canoe and putting it to rights again—could go on an overnight trip while land-lubbers enjoyed the wonderful hikes in the woods and hills surrounding the camp.

A visit from two real live "Mounties", resplendent in their red coats, brought out all the cameras—and

speaking of cameras one may guess that few activities
went unrecorded with the army of T.V. and Radio
crews around the camp, not to mention the ladies and
gentlemen of the Press.

Doe Lake, Ontario

The tropics of the Philippines, the Mountains of
Switzerland, the woods and lakes of Canada—and now
to yet a different scene, the typical English landscape of
Windsor Great Park, generously lent us by our Queen

and Patron for the United Kingdom's "piece" of the World Camp, which brought together 4,000 girls from 68 countries.

Less typical was the English weather, for the sun shone without ceasing throughout those wonderful days. The Clerk of the Weather might well be accused of discriminating in favour of the Guides because the Scout Jamboree at Sutton Coldfield, held at the same time, suffered a monumental thunderstorm! But perhaps this only proved that B.-P.'s spirit was bringing them "Chief's Weather".

At Windsor, every day brought its special excitement. There was the visit of the Queen, who was presented with camping equipment for the Royal children. "They say they know very well how to pitch a tent" she remarked "because they have seen you doing it on television."

Every day there were performances in the arena by different national contingents, the West Indies steel band making a great impression.

There were excursions to see the countryside, and also the Scouts in their vast tented city; there were the World Chief Guide's visits when enthusiasm knew no bounds and was only equalled by the reception given to our President, the Princess Royal. Caps, scarves, belts were flung rapturously into the air as she drove by in a Land Rover to vociferous cheering, and it seems doubtful whether anyone ever again managed to retrieve all her various bits and pieces of uniform.

The sub-camps were all named after places connected with B.-P. s life and all had wonderfully constructed gateways, the most amusing being Stanhope Gardens, where he was born, which had as its centre piece a stork carrying a baby!

The Chinese have a proverb: "It is better to light one small candle than to complain about the dark."

With this thought in mind Guides, past and present, placed lighted candles in the windows of their homes on the evening of Thinking Day 1957, symbolising their gratitude for the past and their hope for the future of the world-wide sisterhood to which they belonged.

Golden Jubilee

The Movement had hardly caught its breath after the great events of 1957 before plans were afoot to celebrate its Golden Jubilee. "We must do something different." Everybody said this but the question was "What?"

South Africa decided on the slogan "Get Another Guider". With more Guiders more Companies and Packs could be started for children of all races who were eager to become Guides and Brownies. So a big publicity and public relations drive was put in hand to explain Guiding to all the people, to tell of its aims and how it set out to achieve them, to show that the girls had fun and at the same time served the community.

The start was a march past of 1,000 girls of all races in Cape Town; next day there were displays in big stores with information desks manned by Guiders. The new uniform, approved by the well-known English designer, Norman Hartnell, was a sign for the fashion conscious that Guides were up-to-date in this respect. Other towns throughout the country organized similar events and the net result was a 25% increase in Guiders and a very large increase in supporters of the Movement.

Australia's emphasis for the year was on adventure, the different States interpreting this according to their own ideas. Exploring Central Australia was one way—flying and driving over the desert, meeting Aborigines, visiting "A Town Like Alice" (known to us through Nevil Shute's book) and having many adventures by the way.

Building the camp fire at the International Year Camp, Pretoria, South Africa in 1965

Canada's idea was to plant a Golden River of Tulips right across their vast land from Atlantic to Pacific—what a glorious sight this must have been when all the flowers were in bloom in the spring!

Finland, through "Operation Heart", provided a heart-lung machine for a hospital to enable treatment to be given to a child suffering from congenital heart disease.

Denmark raised money to buy camp sites all over the country, so that more children could have the joy of experiencing life in the open.

And what about Great Britain? Was there perhaps some part of the programme that had not had sufficient attention paid to it?

"Learning to appreciate the arts is just as important as being a good camper," said one and then another of those people in Headquarters who make decisions. "Drama is perhaps the simplest to understand for the amateur" they continued "as through it we learn something about ourselves, our weaknesses and our strengths, how to express emotion and how to control it. Also it's lots of fun."

If you had been around in 1960 you might have heard girls in all parts of the United Kingdom asking one another "Are you going to Wembley?" and you would be excused for thinking that they had suddenly developed into football fans. But no, "Wembley" for them meant the Festival of Youth in which 1,000 Guides took part and which was the great occasion of the year attended by 36,000 people. The performance began with a colourful "Carnival of Badges" and was followed by "The Journey of Soy".

Soy was not a Guide, but the sort of girl one hopes a Guide might be, for by her steadfastness and adventurous spirit she rescued her (imaginary) country from darkness . . . the darkness caused by temptations that beset the youth of all nations.

Australian Guides raising the flagpole at Glengarry Training Centre
in New South Wales

On a dramatically smaller scale there was TWIGYL.
Twigyl? ?

Theatre Workshop, an International Gathering for
Young Leaders.

"We came from all over the world," wrote a

representative from Austria, "fifty young Leaders from 18—25 years old, interested in the arts, full of anticipation and curiosity about this mysterious adventure. Soon our questions were answered, we heard the story we were going to perform and we were divided into groups.

"The Birthday of the Infanta", this wonderful story by Oscar Wilde, was to be transformed into dance-drama, this was the aim of the ten days' hard work.

The drama group gave the atmosphere of the Spanish court—stiff courtiers and the heartless little Infanta. The dance group brought pleasure and fun to the Infanta with bull-fights, puppets and eastern dancing. The costume and props. group produced the festive but formal picture of the Spanish court.

There is nothing more exciting than working with people who are enthusiastic, who want to create something new of their own. And it became our own.

It was such fun that we did not have much time to sleep; as we worked so hard in the day we could not waste our time sleeping at night, because we wanted to profit as much as possible from being together.

The climax was reached in the performance. Stage fright made us tremble the last afternoon until the curtain rose and we had to show the VIP audience what we had achieved in nine days. It was a success! And we celebrated according to British stage tradition with a big party and a birthday cake and toasts to Guiding.

But it was not the end at all! The Theatre Workshop has given us courage to bring more of the arts into the programme with our own Guides and Brownies and Rangers."

So indeed TWIGYL was a success—for that was the object!

The World Guide Centres

Mexico—land of the Aztecs and of the famous volcano Popocatepetl! How romantic it sounds and how romantic it is for those lucky enough to visit our Cabana.

Cuernavaca is celebrated for Mexican crafts and near this city, 4,000 feet up, is one of the four World Centres where Guides and Girl Scouts can spend their holidays.

Our Cabana at Cuernavaca, Mexico

Our Chalet had proved such a success that the Girl Scouts of the Western Hemisphere were determined to have a similar house in their part of the world, so, with

the approval of the World Committee, they set about
finding a site, raising the required sum of money and
engaging an architect of genius.

Our Cabana is composed of a number of buildings so
cleverly sited that each one has a wonderful view of the
distant mountain range which includes Popocatepetl and
Iztaccihuatl, names commemorating two legendary
lovers whose sad tale was re-enacted at the opening
ceremony in 1957.

The craft room, where the famous Mexican crafts are
taught, is a great attraction and so is the on-going social
service project in nearby villages, while the swimming
pool, given by generous American friends, provides a
splendid leisure time meeting place for girls from all
over the world.

How different is the scene when we move to the Earls
Court district of London! Here is Olave House, named
in honour of the World Chief Guide. Most people spend
only a few nights here for sight-seeing and visiting
friends but some girls studying or working in London
make it their home for a year or more. To celebrate
Diamond Jubilee Year in 1970, however, plans were
made for a London adventure session, the first special
international event of its kind to be held at Olave
House.

This centre was originally called Our Ark and
occupied two little houses in Westminster next door to
the World Bureau. It was launched on to a stormy sea of
world crisis in May 1939, just in time to serve as a
refuge for Guides fleeing from war-torn Europe.

Soon after celebrating its 21st birthday Our Ark
moved to bigger premises, and in 1963 it was re-named
Olave House.

At the same time the World Bureau had outgrown what once seemed ample accommodation, and as the Boy Scouts' World Bureau was moving across the sea to Canada they invited the Guides to take over their building. But don't go looking for the Scout World Bureau in Ottawa—it has since moved back again to Europe and is now to be found in Geneva.

Although Olave House is in central London it has a charming garden, much appreciated on hot summer days, when meals can be eaten out-of-doors. It is a real international centre and has built up its own traditions with special parties to mark the national days of a variety of countries. Incidentally the Guider-in-Charge claims they can provide forty different breakfast dishes!

Sangam is a Sanskrit word meaning "a coming together of rivers" and also "a place of pilgrimage" so it is an appropriate name for our fourth World Guide House where so many girls of different traditions and customs meet together.

This house in Poona, India, suffered many vicissitudes in the building. The foundation stone was laid by Dame Leslie in January 1964, but shortly afterwards the Government of India imposed restrictions on building materials owing to the acute shortage of supplies. Great perseverance and faith were needed to press on with the work, but eventually in 1966 it was opened by Lady Baden-Powell although it was not quite completed.

It is a beautiful building with its arches and cloister-like walk around the central swimming pool, and its Assembly Hall open on all four sides to the winds of heaven.

It was the swimming pool which caused the delay in completing the house, for when digging began a huge rock was found to be barring the way. It could not be blown up with dynamite for fear of wrecking the building, so it had to be chipped away by hand, a lengthy proceeding.

'Know Japan' was the theme of the first international Ranger gathering to be held at Sangam. The two British representatives returned home full of enthusiasm for Japanese culture and eager to instruct their friends in Japanese flower arrangements and the famous Tea Ceremony.

Our Chalet, Olave House, Our Cabana, Sangam—all so different and yet all the same in their friendly, international atmosphere! How fortunate are Guides and Girl Scouts to have a home from home in four different countries.

Service

"I promise that I will do my best . . . to help other people."

Bridging the gap between the "haves" and the "have-nots" is one of the most intractable problems of our time. In spite of the efforts of governments and the big international relief agencies there still remains a great gulf between the rich industrial nations and the developing countries, while even the so-called "affluent societies" have their black spots of poverty and loneliness.

Food, shelter, education, jobs, are desperately needed by many millions, but above all there is the desire for friendship, for the realisation that one is not forgotten and that there are people who care.

Countless service projects, great and small, are being carried out by Guides all over the world, many in co-operation with other organizations, some requiring training in special skills, all demanding reliability and tact in the performance.

Here are just a few examples of such projects taken from accounts that have appeared in *The Council Fire* from time to time.

Guiding Among the Homeless

One winter's day at 3.30 a.m. two Trainers, one

British and one Finnish, met at the railway station in Cologne. They were about to set out on a 500 mile drive with the object of visiting a number of refugee centres and starting Guide Companies and Brownie Packs.

The year was 1955, ten years after the end of the war, when many people thought that the problem of 'displaced persons' had long since been solved.

It is hard for us to imagine the dreariness of these centres, the desolate discomfort of the dwellings, the lack of any kind of entertainment or activity. A typical *lager* (camp) would consist of single-storey wooden huts divided into rooms ten feet square with a door opening on to a dark corridor. Each room would be the home—if one can call it such—of two, three or four persons. Washing facilities would be away in another building. Furniture would amount to a small stove, one or two beds, a table and perhaps three chairs. If one of the occupants were working there might be the luxury of a carpet, a couch and a radio.

The centres housed anything between sixty and six hundred people, with as many as thirteen nationalities speaking thirteen different languages. The children of Brownie and Guide age attended German schools, if they were well enough, so language for them was not a barrier, but the old people were naturally insistent that the younger generation should be brought up in the traditions of their country of origin, even though few of the children could remember any life outside the camp where most of them had been born.

Arriving at a *lager* our Trainers would immediately be surrounded by a swarm of children eager to inspect the car and the interesting new visitors. Organized games, singing and dancing were soon under way, the youngsters entering into the fun with the greatest enthusiasm. After this came the hardest part—finding volunteers willing to train as Leaders.

From the neighbouring camps fourteen young women volunteered to attend the training arranged in a quiet village near Münster to which a Guider from each of the three German Associations had also been invited to act as Patrol Leaders.

This training and other sessions that followed proved highly successful, not only in regard to practical work but also in breaking down national prejudices. Cooking sausages on sticks over an open fire, playing scouting games in the woods and singing—always singing—brought everyone together in friendship.

It seems strange, but it is a fact, that few of the German Guides were aware of the existence of these camps. Once they knew of them, however, they were eager to help.

They started by organizing several big international gatherings for would-be Guides from Poland, Lithuania, Latvia, Estonia and the Ukraine, and they also invited British and Canadian Guides, the children of soldiers serving in Germany. Later on they formed a committee with representatives of all the nationalities to arrange camps (the tented sort, not the refugee kind!) so that the children could get together and make friends.

The giving was not by any means all on one side. It came as a surprise to the refugee children to realise that from the little they possessed they had so much to give—their songs and dances, their talent for making pretty things from odd scraps of material, their ideas and their enthusiasm.

In the Middle East the refugees were even worse off

than those in Germany, who could at least look forward to being re-housed in time.

In the camps in Jordan, Syria, Lebanon and Gaza many of the homeless lived in tents, blazing hot in summer, icy cold in winter. These people had no work, no money, very few possessions and little hope for the future.

This tragic situation was the result of the creation of the new state of Israel, which gave a national home to the Jewish people who had themselves endured exile for hundreds of years.

In one of these camps where a Guide Company was started the girls were determined to get into uniform, like Guides everywhere else, but how could this be achieved? They managed to find some old bits of material which they dyed and made into triangular ties and from some empty sardine tins they cut out their Promise Badges. This was their uniform and they were rightly proud of it.

Some years ago the United Nations Relief and Works Agency for Palestine Refugees set up a Vocational Training Centre in Jordan. Here at Ramallah girls could train as teachers, hairdressers, secretaries, nurses and so on, thus giving them the opportunity to earn a livelihood.

In the course of her travels the Adviser for Associate Membership of the World Association visited the Centre and her account of the splendid work being done there inspired several groups of Guides in different countries to provide the training fees for an 'adopted sister'.

Then in 1964 the Adviser 'was given the honour' as she wrote 'to enrol the girls of the two Guide Companies formed at Ramallah.' When she arrived at the Centre she was greeted with the words 'We feel that you are our mother' and later the Principal told her how much it means to the girls to have sponsors to help them to help themselves.

Before the enrolment, which took place in the presence of a distinguished gathering, the Adviser had time to see the various classes at work and was even given a shampoo and set by the trainee hairdressers!

Of the ceremony she wrote, 'It was a touching moment, especially keeping in mind the background from which these girls come, and reminded me of the universal aspect of Guiding, of all that unites us in spite of differences.'

The re-drawing of national boundaries inevitably causes hardship. When, in 1947, India gained independence and at the same time the sub-continent was divided into two separate countries millions of Muslims, who found themselves living in India, set out to journey to Pakistan, and Hindus from Pakistan set out for India. In the huge refugee camps resulting from this mass migration there were no schools for the children, nor indeed anything to occupy them through the livelong day. How delighted they were when Guide trainers arrived to start companies and packs! The problem was so huge that it might have daunted the bravest and only a small percentage of the thousands of children could be catered for. These few were lucky ones.

The Korean Girl Scouts were just getting going when war devastated their country. One group of thirty girls lost their homes and their families as they fled from the advancing armies, but their Leader managed to find a big marquee which served them for a home in the town they eventually reached—Pusan—and from there they went out to work, helping other refugees in a camp nearby. Their example was such that three troops of Girl Scouts were formed in that place, and now South Korea has a flourishing Girl Scout organization and is a Full Member of the World Association.

World Refugee Year, an attempt by the United Nations to focus attention on this human problem, coincided with the Golden Jubilee Year of the Guide Movement in 1960. This gave the impetus to celebrate fifty years of Guiding by carrying out special service projects with refugees in mind.

How much money was raised will never be known for in most places the work was done in co-operation with other organizations, several thousands of pounds, however, found their way to the World Bureau to further Guiding in refugee centres, and in this way members of the Movement tried to pass on to others some of the fun and happiness they themselves had found through Guiding.

Feeding the Hungry in Rhodesia

In 1965 the Chief Commissioner of Rhodesia received a letter from one of the Division Commissioners describing the desert conditions developing in her area after three years without a drop of rain; dying cattle, failing crops, hungry people, especially children who often walked five miles to school cold and unfed, too under-nourished to be able to concentrate on their lessons.

This Commissioner had obtained some supplies of powdered soup, rich in protein, and her African Guides and Rangers had undertaken the responsibility of mixing this powder with water and serving it to the school children during their morning break. The children's health had improved dramatically and when the Chief Commissioner heard this she was so impressed that she challenged the Rangers, Guides and Brownies of all Rhodesia to an Easter Good Turn, namely to raise enough money so that the good work could continue.

Nigerian Girl Guides helping to build the Cheshire Home in Ibadan

The word got round and soon the money rolled in from outside people as well as from members of the Movement. There was far more than was needed for the original area and soon 3,000 children in 26 schools were getting their daily ration served to them by Guides and Rangers.

With the summer holiday a new campaign started: "Fill the Bin" and everyone went hard at it for the next six weeks. Grocery stores were delighted to co-operate. It was after all good for trade!

A bin was placed in each store and beside it a poster, supplied by headquarters, inviting shoppers to contribute a tin of protein food—fish, meat, dried milk—to feed the hungry. Volunteers collected, packed and transported the food to hospitals and clinics in distant places where it was used to supplement the diet of sick children.

As may easily be imagined underfed children had little or no resistance to common childish diseases, which often proved fatal in their weakened state. But in a school where Guides were serving milk only ten pupils out of 500 came down with measles during an epidemic which ran like wildfire through neighbouring schools.

In one place where the school well dried up, the Guides led the way in carrying 20 gallons of water daily from their homes to mix the drink, and this so impressed the local government officer that he had a new bore-hole sunk. It was certainly a day of rejoicing when a few weeks later the water gushed forth.

Brownies had their part in the scheme, they collected firewood, very scarce in some places, so that water suspected of being impure could be boiled.

This was a truly multi-racial effort, children and grown-ups of all the races working with all their might to make a success of the project, which continued for nearly two years.

A School in Peru

The lure of the big city is the same the world over. Country people hear tell of the bright lights, believe "the streets are paved with gold" and fancy that cushy jobs will fall into their laps like ripe plums. This beautiful dream-life, they think, will take the place of back-breaking dawn-to-dusk toil on the land.

In Peru hundreds of families left their simple life in the mountains to settle in the cities, bringing the problem of under-developed areas congested by people with no training to enable them to earn a living in their new surroundings.

The Government did its best to cope with the shortage of schools and houses and also appealed for help to organizations specialising in leisure time activities.

"This is right up our street," said the Guides and answered the call immediately. With the help of the Government they undertook to build a school in Pamplona where they would take charge of primary education and run a recreation and training centre during the evenings and at week-ends.

This was certainly an ambitious project, but nothing daunted they set to work to raise the large sum required. The news spread and Guides in other countries lent a hand. UNESCO became interested and decided to include the project in its Gift Coupon Scheme, which enables people abroad to buy coupons in their own country for conversion into goods in another country. It reminds one in a way of trading stamps!

A TV programme sponsored by a large store ran a competition with big money prizes in which the competitors were challenged to:

1) secure a piece of land through private donations or a government grant;
2) obtain building materials to the value of 3,830 dollars;
3) carry a message from the President to the TV studio by passing it hand over hand;
4) in front of TV cameras, in three minutes, make a camp gadget from material found only on the site;
5) and lastly, a light-hearted touch, produce a team of five to throw raw eggs into glasses attached to the chests of five Boy Scouts!

History does not relate what the Scouts thought of this caper!

The school today is in running order and is being expanded year by year, the parents enthusiastically supplying some of the labour in gratitude for the classes arranged for themselves in such subjects as first aid, handicrafts and literacy, as well as for the games and sports provided for their children.

Britain's Panorama

Three thousand yards of material, two thousand five hundred reels of cotton, innumerable pieces of leather and felt, hundreds of Guide Magazines—one and a half tons in all—were delivered at Bristol University one fine day in July 1961. Five hundred pairs of willing hands turned the lot into clothing, toys, charts and what-have-you for the Save the Children Fund.

Guests from abroad had enjoyed a week's hospitality before joining British Rangers to explore the country-side as the fifty-eight small groups travelled in leisurely style towards Bristol, making a record of their journey as they went.

New experiences ranged from milking cows to a chance meeting with Princess Margaret in church, from walking up Snowdon to winning a prize at a Carnival.

Arriving at Bristol they got down to the job in hand, not only in the workshops but also helping in old people's and children's homes and at Peter Scott's bird sanctuary at Slimbridge.

The World Chief Guide, passing through England on her way from Denmark to Iceland, dropped in on the party to inspire the Rangers with renewed enthusiasm and attended the camp fire lit by a Greek Ranger in classical dress.

One of the Rangers, with a fine sense of alliteration, wrote: "Freedom, fellowship and friendliness flowered throughout the three weeks in workshops, free time, meals and the Jazz 'n Twist session!"

Exploration, adventure, service—this was Britain's Panorama.

A Forgotten Village in Greece

Try and find Tsapournia on the map of Greece. However diligently you search you will not find her. She is unidentified, desolate, almost non-existent. There, in a huddle of stone hovels 940 metres up a mountainside in Thessaly, live 500 people, completely forgotten.

The inhabitants are all shepherds as there is no arable land. The standard of living is mere survival. There is no sanitation, electricity or running water. The road is almost impassable, there are no newspapers nor any communication with the outside world.

Nine of us arrived there one May morning in 1968 in an army truck, covered with dust and not a little dismayed at the appearance of the village where we were

to spend the next five days. The houses, grey and
forlorn, stood in slushy lanes choked with refuse where
the pigs roamed at random. The villagers stood in groups
and gazed apathetically as we unloaded our belongings.
None lent us a hand.

In true Greek tradition we started with the café,
which is the centre of village social life. No women
come here and our appearance in this man's world was
met with some surprise.

In a few hours the bleak and cheerless café was
completely transformed and in the evening we called
our first meeting. When the villagers began drifting in to
start working on the four kilos of *ouzo* consumed each
night their usual sombre expressions were lightened by a
hint of genuine pleasure.

After this first evening we were getting to know
Tsapournia and its people. It was their feeling of
abandonment that we strove to alleviate. We had come
not only to help them, but to convince them of their
own identity.

There was a church, but the door was barred; there
had not been a priest for ten years. Within everything
was dirty, broken, disintegrating. This was worse than
vandalism, this was the destruction of indifference.

"Is there not a Christian left in Tsapournia?" we
asked ourselves as we battled with the debris.

Three women passing outside peeped in.

"If we go to church the men laugh at us" they said.
But next day they came back and helped.

"What will the men say?" we asked.

"Now that they have seen you, educated girls, coming
here they won't dare open their mouths. But it's a
shame for you to clean our church. From now on we'll

do it ourselves."

The first glimpse of the traditional Greek pride called *filotimo*!

The next day we turned our efforts to the village itself. We spruced up the municipal office and set up an adequately equipped clinic for the visiting doctor. We organized an exhibition of local handcrafts and were amazed at the excellence of the village girls' weaving and embroidery—an undreamed of source of income if they but chose to exploit it. We chatted with the women and tried to give them some practical advice on child-care without insulting their natural pride as mothers and grandmothers.

The graveyard is half-an-hour's climb up the mountain, the graves are ditches dug between the rocks, covered with logs and boulders. Not a cross or a name anywhere. We removed the logs, white-washed the stones and set up crosses painted with the names of the dead, already it looked less stark and forbidding.

Meanwhile other members of our group were working a small miracle on a flat stretch of ground behind the church. This is now a village square, smooth and paved, with wooden benches, a fountain, a children's playground and a monument to the heroic dead.

At first the villagers watched us in amazement, they seemed to think we were stark mad, but gradually they were drawn into the effort, and when the day came for the flag to be raised in the square none in Tsapournia could say others had built it for them. It was their square.

And so it went on till we even began to believe we had accomplished something.

On the last evening we invited a guest speaker to come up from Volos. She took St. Paul's Epistle to the

Corinthians as her text and spoke to the men of Tsapournia on the meaning of love. They listened in silence very moved. At the end a seventy-year-old shepherd, proud of his descent from a famous brigand, and considered 'unsuitable' by the Mayor's wife, rose slowly to his feet.

"I have heard preachers and priests in my time" he said "but you girls have made it all as clear as crystal. But there is one point that puzzles me. Why is it that all those loving feelings disappear when somebody pinches one of my sheep?"

The result was a unique exchange of views between the virtuous lady and the robber's grandson, beneficial to both!

"You remember us" they kept saying "everybody else has forgotten us; they only come before elections and promise things they never mean. They said somebody called 'Common Market' would come and help us, but he never came."

"Till you came we thought nothing could be done" said an old man "but now we know anything can be done with a little caring. Look at our village. We'll never let it get the way it used to be."

"We'll miss you" they said as we scrambled into our truck the next morning "Don't forget us".

Don't worry Tsapournia—we won't.

An International Youth Centre in France

The Guides de France started to build an international youth centre several years ago for boys and girls. For many summers British Rangers have helped in the construction, as a new building is added or an old one redecorated. Youngsters from all over Europe, not necessarily Guides or Scouts, come to lend a hand, and besides the practical work there are animated discussions on every topic of concern to the young.

Then the Rangers go off in small groups on what the French call *Les Routes*. They explore the countryside, help the farmers with the harvest and talk to the people, finding out what life is like in this rural, mountainous area.

The words of a Welsh Ranger who took part in this project in 1963 may perhaps serve as a summing up of all that Guides hope for as they give service to their fellows at home or abroad: 'I remember a remote valley in the Basses Alpes which had been the scene of heavy fighting in the war. There was nothing left to indicate that people had been living in the tiny scattered villages since the Middle Ages and perhaps even before. Every sturdy little house had the rather gauche uncertain look of the newly-built, and the beetle-browed mountains were still disfigured by the slowly crumbling ruins of the old gun emplacements.

Among the kindly, friendly people life went on just as it must always have done . . . even so it will be a very long time before the memory of war disappears from the valley.

One afternoon scrambling through the pine woods, laughing and singing we stumbled quite by accident upon the remains of a bunker still served by its grass-entangled ammunition lines. On a tree nearby hung a rusting helmet and a faded wooden plaque, placed there to honour a handful of the combatants who died rather more spectacularly than the majority of their fellows. We were all suddenly made aware of the criminal waste of life and beauty that was symbolised there, of the impulse to destroy that seems to be an integral part of the nature of man.

". . . *et changer en fleurs tous les cailloux de l'avenir*" is a line stolen from an enchanting Israeli folk-song which caught the imagination of us all—"to change into flowers the stones of the future". We first heard it as we sat grouped around a glowing camp-fire brazier under the cold unwinking brilliance of the stars far above . . .

At Melan I think we all felt that we were creating something, doing our small bit in trying to build a better world founded on hope and companionship instead of suspicion and fear.

Melan is the village of the new hearths, born of the impulse of man to create, an impulse just as old and as powerful as the other impulse of destruction . . . and its symbol is a small twisting flame.

Such projects may perhaps appear very small beside all the chaos and topsy-turviness that exists in our modern world. Yet taken as a whole they could perhaps change the emphasis, if not of our own generation, of generations yet unborn, so that their emblem will become the new flame of friendship rather than a rusting, wasted helmet of war. At least we liked to think so.'

Thinking Day

February 22nd is the joint birthday of the Founder and the World Chief Guide. It was at the 4th International Conference at Camp Edith Macy that somebody suggested that it should be called "Thinking Day" and kept as the World Guide Day everywhere. Since then it has grown in importance as an occasion for special ceremonies in which, often, candles are lit and good wishes exchanged between Guide friends in different countries.

The Founder's memorial, Westminster Abbey with
Thinking Day wreaths

A special service takes place in Westminster Abbey every year on the Saturday nearest to 22nd February. The Abbey doors open at 10 a.m. but long before that Guides and Scouts are standing patiently in line waiting to be admitted. On this great day the ancient building is filled almost to bursting point, with Cubs and Brownies

SERVICE 155

sitting on hassocks alongside the pews, with others standing three and four deep against the walls.

This was certainly the case in 1969, when 22nd February actually fell on a Saturday and marked the World Chief Guide's eightieth birthday. Some people on reaching this age like to retire from active life, but not the Chief. As she said later "We have, praise be, a number of octogenarians still with us whom we might describe as sleeping partners—but I do not sleep!" She certainly does not! That year, 1969, she travelled thousands of miles by plane and car and train, visiting North America for the Scout Jamboree, Finland twice, for the World Conference of both Scouts and Guides, as well as Nigeria, and all in three months. Need one add that wherever she went she made speeches, attended rallies, gave T.V. and Radio interviews and hardly slept in the same bed for two nights running.

So it was lucky for the British that she happened to be in England for her birthday and able to attend the service in the Abbey, where she read the Lesson. It was from St. Paul's well-known Epistle to the Corinthians: 'Though I speak with the tongues of men and of angels and have not charity . . .' Her voice rang out strong and clear; hearing her one could not believe that the speaker was anything but a young woman.

A Penny With Your Thoughts

At the seventh World Conference in Poland a Belgian Guider put forward the idea of 'A penny with your thoughts' and ever since then the giving of pennies—or cents or pesetas or whatever—has been an important feature of Thinking Day ceremonies in all countries, even where the Guides are much worse off than in Britain.

This money is used by the World Association to help Guiding wherever the need is greatest, and the needs grow more urgent with each succeeding year, but happily the response of the Guides who 'have' to those who 'have not' also becomes more generous every year. In 1951 they gave £3,500, in 1968 £36,000. Even so it is not enough to answer all the appeals for help.

In 1967 therefore a new scheme was launched under the rather uninspiring title "Mutual Aid", but nobody could think of a better name. From time to time the World Bureau publishes a leaflet listing a large number of needs ranging in price from a few shillings to hundreds of pounds: pots and pans for a new Guide house; a jeep for an African country; a typewriter for a Latin American country; expenses of a trainer to Asia; the cost of translating a handbook into a local language; the fare for a Leader wishing to take a training course in a more experienced country and so on.

Expensive projects may be taken up by a national organization, or by several jointly, but even a tiny Pack of Brownies can find something within their means.

In 1964 the United Kingdom launched the Guide Friendship Fund to be used mainly, but not exclusively, to help Guiding within the Commonwealth. Up to the end of 1969 forty-six countries had received gifts ranging from cars to sewing machines, as well as money towards building headquarters and for relief in times of disaster caused by hurricanes, floods and earthquakes.

The Fund's scope has now widened to include help to all children whether or not they are Guides. Under the aegis of the Royal Commonwealth Society for the Blind a special "Christmas Good Turn" was undertaken in 1968 for the benefit of blind and partially sighted children in India, Africa and Malaysia. In 1969 the Christmas effort concentrated on providing a "Guide Friendship Nursery" for abandoned children in Jamaica.

Besides all this the Fund contributes generously to the World Association's Mutual Aid scheme.

Tomorrow

The Wind of Change

The wind of change was blowing across the world and of course through the Guide Movement which always reflects changes in the atmosphere.

Certain gentlemen of the national press were asking 'Is Guiding out of date?' and naturally they asked the same question about Scouting—but here we are concerned with the girls.

It is true that the writers of the articles seemed to know very little about the Movement, indeed they had hardly progressed beyond the stage of thinking that the only activity to which Scouts and Guides were passionately addicted was tying knots.

Census figures showed that the number of Guides and Brownies were the highest ever, so it appeared that Guiding was still attractive to the young, but there did seem to be a sad falling away among the over-fourteens.

We can guess at a number of reasons that contributed to this state of affairs. To begin with girls were growing up more quickly, activities that satisfied the fourteen-year-old in previous years seemed now more applicable to the twelve-year-old. In addition schools and other organizations had adopted much of the programme that had been pioneered by the Scouts and Guides in the early days. In the post-war years the opportunities for young people to take up all kinds of sport had increased enormously and the world of entertainment was also competing for attention during out-of-school hours.

There's more to Guiding than knots. Guides in new uniforms rehearsing at the 1969 Folk Festival at Croydon

Besides this one might suppose that a girl who had been a Brownie and then a Guide during perhaps six years would be looking for new interests. We were not too worried about this because so many came back to the Movement as Guiders after a few years.

It is quite true that the Guide programme as it stood embraced a wide field of activities but maybe Guiders and the Guides themselves had got into a rut and were not following their Founder's advice to 'Look wide, and when you think you are looking wide—look wider still.'

The Movement had not remained static through the years; tests and uniform had been up-dated from time to time, but now it was decided that a real shake-up was needed.

A working party was therefore appointed to look into every aspect of the programme and organization, and even into the basic principles. Nothing was to be left out, there were to be no 'sacred cows'.

The Chief Scout had set up his Advance Party to do the same for the Scouts and the two groups met frequently to consult one another and compare notes.

The Working Party started off by asking questions of people outside the Movement as well as of those inside it. Experts of all kinds and various ages were consulted; questionnaires were sent to Guide Companies, Brownie Packs and Ranger units and were published in the Guide magazines; gatherings of Guiders, Commissioners and Trainers were asked for their views and individuals were begged to contribute their ideas. Everyone from the smallest Brownie upwards had a chance to express herself, and of couse many conflicting likes and dislikes came to light. Even the members of the Working Party did not always agree with one another.

Meanwhile experiments in different methods were being carried out by small groups in certain places and reports on their success or otherwise were studied. Studied also were the new handbooks of countries that had recently adopted a new programme, notably those of the United States, France and the Netherlands. There was no doubt about it—Britain was well in the fashion, for the wind of change was blowing through at least eighteen countries at this time.

Excitement grew as the time for the publication of the Working Party's report drew near, and at last there it was: "Tomorrow's Guide". It was read avidly amid cries of joy from some and cries of alarm from others. You can't please everybody.

The Executive Committee had been incarcerated in Foxlease for several days of intensive study, discussion and decision, and all *its* members didn't agree on every single point.

Finally however the New Programme emerged and with it some radical changes. The old standard tests, which were the same for everybody, had been swept away and instead a very flexible Eight Point Programme was introduced adapted for the three sections of Brownie Guides, Guides and Ranger Guides.

By the end of 1969 it was clear that the Eight Point Programme was proving popular and was on the way to achieving the objective of holding the interest of the older girls. In comparing the census figures for 1969 with those for 1968 we find Ranger Units have increased by 502 and individual membership of this Section by over 5,000, while total membership of the Association is the highest ever at 721,991.

You will remember that B.-P. had originally suggested the name "Ranger Guide" to be the complement of "Rover Scout", so the wheel had turned full circle, but the irony of the situation was that at this very moment the Scouts had decided to turn the Rovers into Venture Scouts!

You will note that Brownies had become Brownie Guides, which is what they had always wanted to be, so

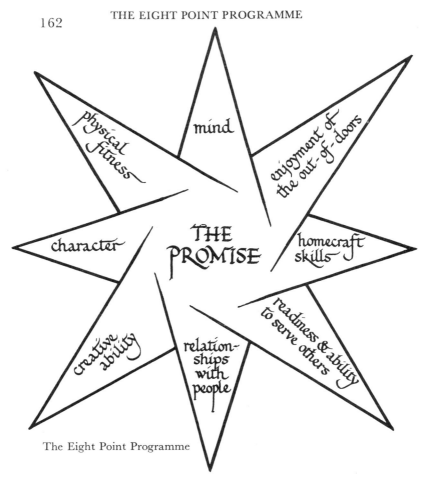

The Eight Point Programme

they were delighted. They had also been given the same Threefold Promise as the Guides— with the exception of the words "Brownie Law" instead of "Guide Law"—and the three-finger Guide Sign as well as a new Promise Badge which showed a Brownie within a Trefoil.

The wording of the Promise and Law had changed; new names appeared in place of familiar old ones, proficiency badges, for instance had become "interest badges", and 'Captain' and 'Lieutenant', 'Brown Owl' and 'Tawny Owl' had disappeared as names at least officially, though it will probably be a long time before they are discarded by Guides and Brownies.

Age grouping had become more flexible; a girl could now join a Ranger group at any time between her fourteenth and sixteenth birthdays, and a Brownie could become a Guide at ten or wait until she was eleven.

In fact "flexibility" was the watchword throughout the whole programme.

However, you can't please everyone, and some Rangers in the Specialised Sections of the Senior Branch were very upset at the proposal to amalgamate them all into the Ranger Guide Service Section, although it was never suggested that they should give up their specialised training.

For many years previously it had been noted that the particular activities of the Land, Sea and Air Rangers and the Cadets had crossed at innumerable points. Sea Rangers were climbing mountains, Air Rangers were sailing, Cadets were asking to take Ranger tests, and hundreds of Rangers of all three sections wanted to train as Guiders, like the Cadets.

If there were only one section for all the older girls any group of Rangers could pursue any activity they had a mind to, and could change to something else if and when they wished; it would make for simplicity and for flexibility.

There was much impassioned discussion on this point

and a good deal of heart-burning, and it was finally agreed that those units that did not want to re-register as Ranger Guide Service Units might continue under their old titles for the time being, but that all new units should be registered under the new scheme.

The storm of protest was reminiscent of 1910 when the Girl Scouts were told to become Girl Guides and give up their Scout hats and badges.

Of course a great many girls welcomed the proposed amalgamation and when the smart new aquamarine shirt made its appearance the enthusiasm became even more marked.

The new handbooks, on which the whole programme hinged, were eagerly awaited. Trainers, who had not seen them (for the contents were a heavily guarded secret) set out to train Guiders who were equally in the dark. As one Trainer remarked "It is the blind leading the blind".

The Americans had been in the same position regarding their new handbooks, but they said that in fact this had worked out splendidly because it had made people think for themselves instead of relying slavishly on the printed word.

When the books did finally appear they reminded one of the *hors d'oevres* in a good French restaurant—hundreds of tasty little dishes to whet the appetite. You can't possibly eat them all so you have to choose carefully the ones that attract you most!

The plan was that every Brownie, Guide, Ranger and Guider should have her own particular handbook on the launching day and many were the gatherings arranged to receive the consignments on 18th March, 1968. 1,237,000 were printed and something like half had to be distributed in towns and villages throughout the United Kingdom.

For the first time in its history the Association under-estimated a mammoth task. On the 17th March telephone lines were red-hot, Guiders drove furiously round the countryside hunting parcels said to be on their way, others rushed to Headquarters in search of their orders.

Sad to relate some consignments did not reach their destination on the Day of Days, and some places got only a few token copies, but in the end everyone received her handbook and in reading it forgot her initial disappointment.

So Guiding got a new look—at least so far as the super-structure was concerned, basically it remains the same. Guides still accept the Promise and Law as the corner stone of the Movement, they still seek adventure and are on the look-out for ways of giving service.

Where once eyebrows were raised at the sight of daringly exposed ankles, albeit modestly clothed in woollen stockings, nowadays bare knees hardly evoke a flicker of an eyelash. Camping and hiking are no longer considered unsuitable activities for delicate females, and who would now dare to repeat the slogan of another age: "Children should be seen and not heard"? Miss Agnes Baden-Powell's emphatic statement that "The Girl Guides have nothing whatever to do with the Boy Scouts and are not allowed out after dark" echoes strangely down the years. Foreign travel is no longer the perogative of the rich, and nobody is surprised if a girl goes in for mountain climbing or even football!

As for service the earliest Guides saw their only chance of helping others in "bringing in the wounded

Ranger ski rescue patrol at Glenshee, Scotland

from the battlefield", though Rangers and Venture
Scouts in Scotland seem in the direct line of descent in
bringing in the wounded from the ski-slopes during
week-ends in the winter season.

In some ways today's Eight Point Programme—in its
flexibility, in its renewed emphasis on the patrol as the

unit for work and play, in its encouragement of individual initiative—has returned to B.-P.'s original conception of the game. Paradoxically in becoming 'oh-so-up-to-date' we have turned back to our beginnings.

Programmes were not the only thing affected by the wind of change. As the years rolled on many countries, particularly in Africa and the Caribbean, were attaining independence and officially severing the ties between themselves and their mother countries. So far as Guiding was concerned this meant that they were now able to become direct members of the World Association instead of being represented by the mother country, Britain, Belgium or France as the case might be.

When a much-loved daughter leaves home to marry or pursue a career she does not cut herself off from her parents, and so it is in our Movement; the happiest relationships exist between the Guides of the former mother country and her erstwhile Branch Associations who are now managing their own affairs.

In 1956 there were 28 Full Member Countries and seven Associate Members. By 1970, the year of the Diamond Jubilee, the number had grown to 50 Full Members and 37 Associate Members. Besides this the United Kingdom had still over 50 Branch Associations and there were over 30 countries working to attain membership in the future.

So the World Association grows in strength from year to year.

Diamond Jubilee
The first World Conference to take place in Asia was held in Japan in 1966 and it was here that plans were

made for Diamond Jubilee Year in 1970—plans, that is, on World level, for of course countries would organise their own national celebrations.

Thoughts went back to Centenary Year and 'The World Camp in Pieces'. This time it was decided, after much discussion, to have gatherings in different parts of the world for Rangers and young Guiders.

Canada, Jamaica, Japan and the United Kingdom offered to act as hostesses and in due course dispatched invitations to all 87 Member Countries of the World Association.

The United Kingdom decided to call their gathering 'Argosy', a poetical word for a merchant ship bearing a cargo of treasures. The name also recalls the Argonauts, the legendary Greek heroes who set out in search of the Golden Fleece.

This seemed an appropriate title for an international event to which the participants would bring their talents and set out to explore the world of arts—painting, music, drama, architecture, photography and crafts.

One hundred visitors from abroad were invited to join one hundred British at Birmingham, where the staff of its famous art centre were to give support to the venture. Unfortunately not so many were able to accept.

With the final exhibition of the work accomplished it was planned that each of the British would take home an overseas guest for a week of relaxation.

The big national event was once more a splendid pageant at Wembley in which 1,000 performers were to take part. The first half, called 'Diamond Circus' presented Guiding in its various aspects, while the second half was to be a theatre workshop production called 'Images and Reflections—an Improvisation'.

Religious services of thanksgiving were planned throughout the country and many local camps to which Guides from abroad were invited. . . The slogan for the year was "Three Cheers", encouraging every member to cheer up another person, a place, and herself!

Since 1910 the century has been punctuated with special anniversaries, each one marked by memorable occasions. No doubt many of the younger ones among us look forward to celebrating a hundred years of Guiding. I wonder if the chief event of 2010 will be an expedition to the moon to visit the Moon-Guides?

The Happiness of Tomorrow

The game which Baden-Powell gave to the children of the world so long ago is being played in much the same form today by over sixteen million boys and girls; and nobody knows how many millions have passed through the movement during the sixty years of its existence.

It has stood the test of time because Scouting began, not as a theory worked out on paper, but as the result of a man giving back to the children of another generation the fun and friendship and ideals of his own boyhood and youth.

An old Hindu proverb says "What you do today is the happiness of tomorrow", and the future of Guiding and Scouting lies in the hands of the girls and boys of today.

It is up to them to play the game as it is meant to be played; to stretch out the left hand of friendship to their brothers and sisters across the sea; to keep alive the Guide and Scout spirit as they grow older; and to hand it on to their successors.

If they do this in their millions, the world will surely be a happier place.

Appendix

Members of the World Association
of Girl Guides and Girl Scouts in 1970

Full Members	*Year Joined*	*Full Members*	*Year Joined*
Argentina	1957	Korea (South)	1957
Australia	1928	Lebanon	1954
Austria	1957	Liechtenstein	1948
Belgium	1928	Luxembourg	1928
Brazil	1930	Malaysia	1960
Canada	1928	Mexico	1948
Ceylon	1950	Monaco	1960
China, Republic of	1963	Netherlands	1928
Colombia	1954	New Zealand	1928
Denmark	1928	Nigeria	1960
Finland	1928	Norway	1928
France	1928	Pakistan	1948
Germany, Federal Republic	1950	Panama, Republic of	1952
Ghana	1960	Peru	1960
Greece	1934	Philippines	1946
Guatemala	1957	South Africa	1928
Haiti	1946	Spain	1957
Iceland	1928	Sweden	1928
India	1928	Switzerland	1928
Iran	1963	Tanzania	1963
Ireland	1932	Trinidad & Tobago	1963
Israel	1954	United Arab Republic	1928
Italy	1946	United Kingdom	1928
Jamaica	1963	United States of America	1928
Japan	1952	Venezuela	1960

Associate Members	Year Joined	Associate Members	Year Joined
Barbados	1969	Kuwait	1966
Bolivia	1966	Liberia	1966
Botswana	1969	Libya	1966
Central African Republic	1963	Madagascar	1963
Chile	1957	Malta	1966
Congo (Brazzaville)	1963	Paraguay	1966
Congo (Kinshasa)	1963	Portugal	1963
Costa Rica	1946	Rhodesia	1969
Cyprus	1960	Sierra Leone	1963
Dahomey	1963	Singapore	1966
Dominican Republic	1969	Sudan	1957
Ecuador	1966	Swaziland	1969
El Salvador	1960	Thailand	1963
Ethiopia	1966	Togo	1963
Gambia	1966	Uganda	1963
Guyana	1969	Uruguay	1966
Ivory Coast	1963	Viet-Nam (South)	1966
Jordan	1963	Zambia	1966
Kenya	1963		

The photographs in this book appear by courtesy of the Girl Guides Association, the Girl Scouts U.S.A. and the World Association of Girl Guides and Girl Scouts, except the frontispiece, which was supplied by the Winnipeg Free Press.

Bibliography

de Beaumont, M. *The Wolf that Never Sleeps*
        (Girl Guides Association)
Choate, A.H., and Ferris, H. *Juliette Low and the Girl Scouts*
        (Girl Scouts U.S.A.)
Kerr, R. *The Cruise of the Calgaric*
        (Girl Guides Association)
        The Story of a Million Girls
        (Girl Guides Association)
        The Story of the Girl Guides
        (Girl Guides Association)
Liddell, A. *The First Fifty Years*
        (Girl Guides Association)
Stewart Brown, P. *All Things Uncertain, the story of the G.I.S.*
        (Girl Guides Association)
Synge, V. *Royal Guides*
        (Girl Guides Association)
The Story of the Four World Centres
        (World Association of Girl Guides and Girl
        Scouts)

Biennial and Triennial Reports of the World Association

The Council Fire, the Quarterly Magazine of the World
Association

Index